English: American Style

*How Americans
Invented Themselves and
Their Language*

Jeffrey McQuain

MJF BOOKS
NEW YORK

Published by MJF Books
Fine Communications
322 Eighth Avenue
New York, NY 10001

English: American Style
LC Control Number 2002106255
ISBN 1-56731-538-0

Previously published by Random House in 1999 as *Never Enough Words:
How Americans Invented Expressions as Ingenious, Ornery, and Colorful
as Themselves*

This edition published by arrangement with Random House Information
Group, a division of Random House, Inc

Manufactured in the United States of America on acid-free paper ∞

MJF Books and the MJF colophon are trademarks of Fine Creative Media,
Inc.

BG   10   9   8   7   6   5   4   3   2   1

To my brother, Dan

The United States themselves are essentially the greatest poem.

—WALT WHITMAN

CONTENTS

Contents

THE FIRST ROUNDUP
ACKNOWLEDGMENTS

On National Dictionary Day in 1985, Representative Bill Green of New York took to the floor of the United States Congress and read into *The Congressional Record* of October 16 this list of assorted Americanisms:

Champ, geek, hoagie, gizmo, scuba, snafu, beeline, thinktank, clipboard, movie, cloudburst, stevedore, sidewalk, freightcar, French toast, Canadian bacon, Chinatown, English muffin, chow mein, chicken à la king, caramba, cloverleaf, coffee table, preempt, paycheck, riproaring, ripsnorting, shovelhead, teddy bear, internal revenue, sideburns, belly flop, letterman, jigsaw, bathtub, barbeque, jumbo, babysitter, chili, lacrosse, teepee, roughneck, floozy, Mickey Mouse, smog, catnap, coyote, crackerjack, and of course, caucus.

After completing the list, Congressman Green revealed his source by saying, "Thanks to David Guralnik, editor-in-chief of *Webster's New World Dictionary,* for supplying us with

14,000 Americanisms, in addition to the small sample listed above."

Nobody can write or speak on the subject of Americanisms without building upon the work of the many word watchers who have gone before. From the earliest colonial days, Americans have been interested in and intrigued by the language of the United States. The names of the multitude of experts who have studied and defined its words form a litany of lexicographers, from Noah Webster and John Russell Bartlett to Mitford M. Mathews and the continuing work of Frederic G. Cassidy.

Before a list of names of the many others deserving acknowledgment as well as thanks, a brief mention should be made of the difficulty in using absolutes about language. ROUNDUP, for instance, sounds like an Americanism, based on the western practice of gathering or driving livestock. In the nineteenth century, however, the term was apparently developed independently in Australia as well as America. Neither can anybody make absolute claims about first usage or the dating of terms, because subsequent discoveries of earlier use are always possible. What is certain, however, is that the words discussed in this work as Americanisms have been enjoyed or favored or popularized in the United States, even though some of these terms may have originated in other parts of the world.

"I have fallen in love with American names," wrote the poet Stephen Vincent Benét, and in the compilation of this book, the names of present-day word experts deserve special thanks: John and Adele Algeo, who recently retired from collecting new words for *American Speech;* Cynthia and Robert Barnhart; David Barnhart; Frederic G. Cassidy and Joan Hall of the *Dictionary of American Regional English;* Robert L. Chapman, the slanguist who revised *Roget's Thesaurus;* Tom Dalzell; Paul Dickson; Frederick C. Mish of Merriam-Webster; Father James B. Simpson, compiler of *Simpson's*

Contemporary Quotations; Anne H. Soukhanov, the author of *Word Watch,* whose revision of Stuart Berg Flexner's work has been published as *Speaking Freely;* and particularly William Safire of *The New York Times,* who guided me in researching his "On Language" column and introduced me to the endless wonders of word watching.

Assistance was also sought from every state's historical society. Particularly helpful were the following: John L. Ferguson, state historian with the Arkansas History Commission; Jeem Trowbridge of the Bangor Historical Society in Maine; Nancy Nott of the Hawaiian Historical Society; Christine Brady of the Idaho State Historical Society; Professor Edward D. Ives of the Maine Folklife Center at the University of Maine; Virginia H. Smith of the Massachusetts Historical Society; Steve Nielsen of the Minnesota Historical Society; the Mississippi Department of Archives and History; Marie Concannon of the State Historical Society of Missouri; Wendell Tripp of the New York State Historical Association; Ed Shoemaker of the Oklahoma Historical Society; Laura Carter of the Western History Collections of the University of Oklahoma; W. K. McNeil of the Ozark Folk Center in Arkansas; and Cindy L. Brown of the Wyoming State Archives.

The author also wishes to express personal thanks for inspiration and guidance to family, friends, and teachers: Genetta McQuain for helping with word files and Dan McQuain for helping with computer files; Mildred Kline; Virginia and Robert McQuain; June and Mark Carson and in memory of Scott Carson; Ruth and Lois Dolly; Lynda J. Foro of Doing Things for Animals, headquartered in Sun City, Arizona; Professor Stanley Malless of Simpson College in Iowa; Dr. Charlotte Fallenius; David Feldman, author of the "Imponderables" books; Steven and Susan Koppe; Professor Robert Feldman of the University of Wisconsin at Oshkosh; Mary Tonkinson of *The Shakespeare Quarterly;* Ann Elise Rubin of *The New York Times;* Professor Barbara Stout of Montgomery College in Rockville, Maryland; Marguerite Coley; Lynn Karpen; Professor Alden Wood; Elizabeth P. Gibbens; Lynn Lawrence; the Reverend Jeanne Klauda and the congregation of North Bethesda United Methodist Church in Maryland; my inexhaustible agent, David Hendin; and my mentor at The American University, Professor Thomas F. Cannon, Jr., for his remarkable lectures on the history of the language.

At Random House, Sol Steinmetz deserves special gratitude for instigating the project, ably followed in the task by Wendalyn Nichols, editorial director of Random House Dictionaries. Other valuable assistance at Random House has been provided by Jesse Sheidlower, senior editor, Amy Warner, editorial assistant, and Michael Burke, copy editor.

Quotations featuring Americanisms over the centuries are included throughout this book. These quotations represent an ever-enlarging sea of America's voices from colonial times to the present: the writers and reporters, editors and orators, diarists and discoverers who have made the American language as rich and varied as it is today. The inclusion of the quotations is meant to help the reader "hear" those original and largely anonymous voices. To that end, the original spelling and punctuation have been preserved throughout as much as possible.

To these knowing and unknowing contributors goes the majority of gratitude for *English: American Style*.

INTRODUCTION
ENOUGH, ALREADY?

$\mathcal{N}$oah Webster, the greatest maker of American dictionaries, suddenly found himself at a loss for words. In the early nineteenth century, he had asked Basil Hall, a naval officer from England, to explain why he considered all American coinages unworthy. "Because," Captain Hall replied, with British finality, "there are enough words already."

Hall was not alone in his disdain for America's influence on the English language. In fact, not everybody has found cause to celebrate the American language or the American character. The first reports of an American dialect were made by British visitors, who denounced it as "barbarous," a tongue filled with "improprieties and vulgarisms." In 1839, a novelist visiting from England sniffed that "It is remarkable how very debased the language has become in a short period in America." A generation earlier, Samuel Johnson, the greatest maker of British dictionaries, had expressed a similar opinion of our national character. "I am willing to love all mankind," Johnson said, "except an American."

For much of our nation's history, it seems, the British have been fighting the American evolution. The New World may have demanded the new word, but innovation was not readily welcomed, even on this side of the Atlantic. British wordsmiths became infuriated by America's prominent use of MAD in the sense of "angry" rather than "insane" (although there was precedence for the former use in British English); Thomas Jefferson found himself belittled for his 1781 coinage of BELITTLE, and lengthy diatribes against the American adjective LENGTHY tried ineffectually to prevent its spread. James Fenimore Cooper tasked his countrymen for their "turgid abuse of terms." Cooper's critics, in turn, have taken satisfaction in pointing out his misuse, in *The Last of the Mohicans,* of the word WISHTONWISH; the novelist used that Chinook Indian name to identify a whippoorwill when it actually refers to a prairie dog.

But another sentiment soon began to be heard across the land. The growth of the American character—richly reflecting its many facets of independence and indignation, passion and prejudice—was helping to produce a new language, an English more striking and flexible than the reserved mother tongue had ever sounded. And as the American personality began to spread, so did the national ability to find just the right words.

"Americans are going to be the most fluent and melodious-voiced people in the world," Walt Whitman rhapsodized before the Civil War, "—and the most perfect users of words."

From rhapsody to rap, the American language has produced thousands of terms beyond existing English words, and writers have long celebrated the richness of America's vocabulary. Excited by the promise of the land and the language, Whitman added a prediction to his praise, tying the growing speech to the character of the speakers. "The new world, the new times, the new people, the new vistas," the poet wrote in 1856, "need a new tongue according—yes, what is more, they will have such a new tongue—will not be satisfied until it is evolved."

TALKING TALL

That evolution began long before Walt Whitman learned to speak American and continues more than a century after his death. Whitman himself, however, might have stumbled over the Americanisms in a southern newspaper editorial that called the federal government "teetotaciously exflunctified."

Nowadays the most fluent of American speakers would also have trouble understanding that editorial, which appeared in 1840 and used an expression that was apparently familiar back then, already in print for almost a decade. TEETOTACIOUSLY is simply "totally," with extra syllables added. EXFLUNCTIFIED, a stretched version of the slang "exflunct," means "worn out." Used together, the two words are a perfect example of talking tall.

Tall talk, a mouthful of unmistakably American language, has grown as much by chance as by design. The tall tales of the American frontier required tall talk, bountiful boasting based on mile-long words that covered the countryside with hyperbole. The nation's pioneers found that creative wording provided as big a challenge as sharpshooting, leading Davy Crockett himself to brag, "I can outspeak any man!"

Imported or homegrown, pioneering words seemed magically to appear in America whenever new meanings needed to be expressed. If English words proved inadequate, our forebears found ways to adapt or invent what they needed. The rapid production of these terms caused many words of yesterday's Americans to come and go, making many of these inventions sound odd or foreign to today's speakers.

These American words, like the American character, have

undergone some swift and surprising changes during the last four centuries. Expressions both local and national have combined to make the language of the United States as varied as its inhabitants. Charting the history and progress of that language offers insight into what the national identity has been and reveals where it may ultimately be headed.

With fading and forgotten treasures in its wealthy store of words, America's speech continues to expand uncontrollably. Behind every American word lies a story, and those stories—some funny, some surprising, some moving—tell tales of America's times and America's people. A careful dissecting of the national character reveals the quirks and qualities that enliven this country's coinages and helps explain why we choose the words we use. As the most revealing record of the national character, in fact, the American language points back to aboriginal Americans and forward to the cyberspace race.

UNITED STATING

Ironically, many of the new words derogated in Britain as "Americanisms" were actually British in origin.

WAMBLECROPPED, for instance, is an adjective that started in Britain as a sixteenth-century term for a stomachache. It came from the verb "wamble," which means "to feel nausea," with "cropped" perhaps from the phrase "crop up," meaning "to occur." While "wamblecropped" failed in England, it flourished here as a northern term for "ill" and a southern term for "drunk."

Eager to sever connection to all things British, the founders of the new country were uncertain about retaining the mother tongue. For a brief time they even considered a proposal that the official American language should be Greek. The suggestion, however, was sensibly quashed when a patriot pointed out that "It would be more convenient for us to keep the language as it is and make the English speak Greek." The British remained unmoved by the suggestion.

Meanwhile Captain Hall's charge of having "enough words already" failed to persuade the tall talkers. America's language proved to be something organic, with new expressions growing freely alongside existing English words. Along with these fast-starting phrases and coinages, a new term for the language itself became necessary.

AMERICAN LANGUAGE was not the first choice; in fact, in the seventeenth century that phrase referred not to English but to American Indian languages. As the collective term for the varied tongues of the native tribes in the New World, it was based on AMERICA, the name assigned by mapmakers in honor of Amerigo Vespucci, the Italian navigator who died in 1512 and who never set foot on American soil. At the turn of the nineteenth century, "American language" (later used by H. L. Mencken as the title for his monumental study of America's words) came into its own as a term for American English, already known in the eighteenth century as AMERICAN TONGUE or just AMERICAN. The twentieth century has tried unsuccessfully to add AMERICANESE.

In the century after the nation was established, UNITED STATES was another term for the language spoken and written throughout the country. In 1879, an Iowa historian expressed a sentiment still powerfully felt by those favoring American English as the official language: "There should be a law compelling railroad people to speak United States." From that usage came TO TALK UNITED STATES, a verb phrase meaning "to use direct or plain language." An 1883 word watcher observed that "Architects are still sometimes exhorted to talk United States," much as lawyers and doctors nowadays are urged to drop their jargon and speak plainly.

And the evolution of our words continues, as well as our language battle with Britain. Throughout the twentieth century, British commentators have continued to frown upon American usage. In response, the legislature of Illinois took steps to separate American permanently from the British variety of English; a formal act of 1923 announced, "The official language of the State of Illinois shall be known hereafter as the American language, and not as the English language."

OUT OF CHARACTER

Proponents of the American tongue from yesteryear have occasionally gone too far. During the nineteenth century, Edgar Allan Poe criticized a poet's efforts for "willful murders . . . on the American of President Polk." Unfortunately, a rallying cry of "the President's American" somehow lacks the ring of "the King's English."

The American language, however, does succeed in reflecting the traits of the American character. From native words to current coinages, our vocabulary demonstrates both the strengths and weaknesses of the national personality, from boldness and creativity to conformity and restlessness. It is a language of the spirit, of the mind, and of the heart.

No one knows exactly how many American words have come and gone in the national vocabulary, and there is only speculation about why some of these strange and colorful terms failed to thrive.

Weird words like ANTIFOGMATIC and CONFISTICATE were formed by extending earlier English words that remain in the language. For instance, "antifogmatic" began two centuries ago as a synonym for "rum." Thought to work wonders against the dampness of cold and foggy weather, "antifogmatic" borrowed the medical ending "-matic," found also in "rheumatic," to make this strong drink sound like medicine. The name fooled nobody; although the humorous word can still be found in the latest edition of the *Oxford English Dictionary,* it has died out. Some drinkers, however, still prefer to call a stiff one ANTIFREEZE. Equally old is "confisticate," "to take away," which on its initial appearance was regarded as "vulgar." This extension of CONFISCATE has also lasted into the twentieth century and is included in the first volume of the *Dictionary of American Regional English,* or *DARE.*

From Portland, Maine, to Portland, Oregon, the growth of the American personality has been reflected by the growth of its language, and playfulness has always played a part. Americans, for instance, have long played with the sound of words, naming whippoorwills or katydids after the sounds they make. With characteristic humor, our ancestors named a LAWYER BIRD for its long bill (or, in the words of an ornithologist, "from its perpetual clamour and flippancy of tongue"). Also catchy is a fish called the LAKE LAWYER, from reports of its "ferocious looks and voracious habits."

Sometimes an American word's formation has practically defied description. For instance, Frederick W. Hodge's 1907 guide to Indian terms offers this convoluted explanation of the name SENECA: "the Anglicized form of the Dutch enunciation of the Mohegan rendering of the Iroquoian ethnic appellative 'Oneida.' " For the most part, American words have etymologies that are easier to determine, although little is known about how popular some of these words became.

Beyond newspapers and humorous stories, in fact, there are few clues about how widespread was the use of many of yesterday's words. The late American lexicographer Stuart Berg Flexner once explained the unpredictable appeal of these terms: "Certain words just catch the public imagination for a time, and those are the words used in place of what was popular before. As something became older or was superseded, replacement synonyms came gradually into use. You rarely hear a car referred to as a 'machine' anymore."

HAPPY HUNTING GROUNDS

"A word is dead/When it is said,/Some say," wrote the poet Emily Dickinson more than a century ago, adding, "I say it just/Begins to live/That day." Her sentiment, however accurate, only starts to explain the mysterious death or disappearance of a wealth of American words.

Nobody can pinpoint the day and time that a word ceases to be. There exists no linguistic terminator, much less a smoking gun next to the dictionary. Many of these native terms sound strange and yet are strangely familiar, long-lost relatives to other words still used.

In the stories to come, America's language will be observed from the earliest frontier words of a PATHFINDER (an 1840 coinage by James Fenimore Cooper) to the latest frontier words of the Pathfinder mission to Mars. The older and less familiar words lead eventually to the latest computer terms, government acronyms, and body language, including the modern reversal of the "thumbs up" sign. Each chapter offers a survey of the memorable terms out of America's past, from oaths and euphemisms to clichés and exaggerations, as signals of America's character.

Much like the history of America, the country's coinages have also occasionally reflected poorly on shameful practices, particularly those of slavery and wartime relocation. These word histories are also included here, because they have played a significant part in the panorama of American life.

The treatment of the American Indian, for example, requires a note on the choice of terminology. NATIVE AMERICAN is felt by many to be more culturally sensitive (INDIAN came from the mistaken notion that the early European discoverers had found a western route to India). Others prefer the more accurate ABORIGINAL AMERICAN, noting that anybody born in America would by definition be a "native American." Many tribal leaders, however, prefer AMERICAN INDIAN, which is the term they recommended for the Smithsonian Institution's planned Museum of the American Indian.

As a result, these terms will be varied throughout the book in recognition of the unsettled linguistic issue. Also, for the sake of accuracy, some of the quotations represent the racist and sexist attitudes evident when the words were used. As often as possible, the quotations retain the original spellings of their sources to reflect more accurately the extent to which the language has changed over the centuries.

Countless studies of America's words are available, but none before has attempted to offer a systematic explanation of why we say what we say. Earlier in this century, the folklorist Constance Rourke tied American character to the development of American humor, and in 1920 the philosopher George Santayana linked America's opinions to such characteristics as our "native good will, complacency, thoughtlessness, and optimism." Here, however, is the first full-blown book on the personality of America's language.

Constantly subjected to change, the American language as well as the American character has grown fast and furiously since the nation's earliest days. Accompanying the chapters that follow are extensive lists of words testifying to the wealth of our wording. Sometimes, though, the development of these words has happened so quickly that opposing influences came into conflict. For example, directness and indirectness have both played a part in the formation of America's expanding expressions. Such conflict, however, is not unexpected.

More than a century ago, Walt Whitman could have been commenting on America's language when he asked, "Do I contradict myself?" The poet's answer to that rhetorical question was telling: "Very well then I contradict myself,/(I am large, I contain multitudes.)" The multitudes of truly American words and phrases owe their rawness and richness to all the complementary and contradictory traits that have helped constitute the American character.

Americana

AMERICAN TURTLE an eighteenth-century forerunner of the submarine, invented by David Bushnell, a Connecticut farm boy who graduated from Yale in 1775

AMERICAN REPUBLIC a more accurate term than "democracy," used for two centuries as a synonym for the United States (also known since 1783 as the "American Empire")

AMERICAN PRIDE an obsolete term, used in 1784 for a scarlet-flowered plant found on riverbanks

AMERICAN NIGHTINGALE another obsolete term used two centuries ago to designate a bird more often known by its call, the "whippoorwill"

AMERICAN PESTILENCE the 1811 term used for an outbreak in Philadelphia of "yellow fever," later called by Noah Webster the "American plague"

AMERICAN BEAUTY a nineteenth-century term applied first to a juicy variety of apple and later to a cultivated rose with dark pink to crimson petals

AMERICAN BOTTOM used since the early 1800s, the term for a stretch of level farmland on the bank of the Mississippi River in southwestern Illinois

AMERICAN BOWLS another name for bowling; Albert Barrerè and Charles G. Leland's 1889 slang dictionary explained, "The game was originally nine pins; but the Blue Laws of Connecticut having forbidden that game, the astute sons of the Puritans added a pin, and made the game, ten pins, or as it is now called 'American bowls'. "

AMERICAN PLAN an 1856 term still used for a hotel arrangement that provides a room and three meals each day, contrasted with the lack of meals in the "European plan"

AMERICAN WAY a nineteenth-century term, frequently used in the negative ("not the American way"), for patriotic principles embodied in a cliché long familiar to "Superman" fans: "truth, justice, and the American way"

PERSONALLY SPEAKING

The American Spirit

CHAPTER 1

INDEPENDENCE

The American spirit has always shown itself to be independent in the coining of words and the constructing of phrases. Even the first president exercised his independence in finding the most memorable phrasing. "Nothing short of independence, it seems to me, can possibly do," George Washington wrote during the Revolutionary War. "A peace on other terms would, if I may be allowed the expression, be a peace of war."

From the Declaration of Independence to Ralph Waldo Emerson's famous 1841 essay "Self-Reliance," America's users of words have long celebrated the ability to go it alone. A new world called for new words and new ways to use old words. Just as colonists called for independence from the tyranny of British rule, they also sought freedom of choice to find an American voice.

Independence is perhaps the single most valuable trait in establishing that American voice, particularly in the language's emphasis on the need for self-reliance. A proverbial saying like PADDLE YOUR OWN CANOE has long indicated the value of being able to move about or work independently.

That American proverb is still heard in an extended version: "Love many, hate few, always paddle your own canoe."

Another old-time term for the importance of independence is the 1840s phrase WORK YOUR OWN ASH-HOPPER, referring to a funnel-shaped container for catching and emptying ashes. Equally unfamiliar to the modern user is the urge for independence in CHOP YOUR OWN ICE, a similar call for personal responsibility. Before the election of 1904, one newspaper editorialized, "Do not think that Teddy Roosevelt is making any mistake in chopping his own Presidential ice."

As the primary attribute of the American character, independence is still being sought throughout the nation. For instance, the latest trend at American colleges involves pledging to stop students from alcohol abuse. Recently, members of several fraternities at the University of Virginia signed a document promoted as a "declaration of independence from alcohol."

NEW WORLD ORDER

Even the earliest Europeans to visit the New World tried to watch their words carefully.

In 1585, the British scientist Thomas Harriot visited the attempted colony of Roanoke, located in what is now North Carolina, and penned *A Briefe and True Report of the New Found Land of Virginia*. Published in 1590, this descriptive work was divided into three parts, including the products of the colony that could be exported to England and, as Harriot wrote, "greatly profit our owne countrey men . . . which commodities for distinction sake, I call merchantable." Harriot was not the coiner of MERCHANTABLE, which dates back to the fifteenth century in England, but that word in his narrative was probably the first example of early American word choice.

What is now identified as EARLY AMERICAN was, of course, not known by the name at that time. Much as World War I was denominated "the Great War" until the onset of a Second World War, colonial times did not constitute "early American" back then. In fact, that phrase came into use only a century ago as a modifier for the furniture and customs of the British colonies. In 1895, a periodical advertised "early American paintings at the Metropolitan Museum," and a 1922 issue of *Country Life* indicated that "Furniture from the workshop of Duncan Phyfe holds distinctly a place of its own in the history of early American utilitarian art."

By the time of the arrival of the first English settlers, the American language was already starting to flourish. Earlier travelers had already come into contact with the natives of what visitors called the New World, and the languages of those natives included words that would become part of the American English vocabulary. Certainly the language of the English settlers was already replete with words and phrases appropriate to the Old World. The circumstances of relocating from a heavily populated country to what seemed largely a wilderness led to the necessity of new words for new situations.

Not until after 1780, though, did the Reverend John Witherspoon begin the study of America's words. A Scottish clergyman who relocated to America and became college president of Princeton, Witherspoon expressed an attitude toward the new language that was less than enthusiastic. In describing eight classes of errors committed by Americans, Reverend Witherspoon explained his dismay: "I have heard in this country, in the senate, at the bar, and from the pulpit, and see daily in dissertations from the press, errors in grammar, improprieties and vulgarisms which hardly any person of the same class in point of rank and literature would have fallen into in Great Britain." To his view, the American language was a trap to be avoided by careful usage. He looked upon "fellow countrymen" as a redundancy not to be tolerated, and he seemed especially angered about the still-popular use of "mad" to mean "angry."

Today the Reverend Witherspoon is remembered as the undisputed coiner of AMERICANISM. Other writers of the times, though, were equally inventive with variations of the name AMERICA. After serving as the first Chief Justice of the Supreme Court, John Jay wrote in 1797 that "I wish to see our people more AMERICANIZED, if I may use that expression; until we feel and act as an independent nation, we shall always suffer from foreign intrigue." Longer phrases, such as "the American language" and "American English," entered the lexicon a decade later, but it was "Americanism" that set the standard for America's words as a category separate from the British English that preceded.

Into that list of Americanisms may be entered a number of words popularized from the days of colonial America onward. These early Americanisms, many formed from British words, came into the language before the Declaration of Independence. Not even that name, in fact, was sacrosanct. Some contemporaries of Thomas Jefferson preferred to refer to his document as the "Declaration of INDEPENDENCY."

COLONIAL COINAGE

Colonists largely built upon the existing vocabulary, but new circumstances required some independently developed expressions.

As early as 1616, Captain John Smith used NEW ENGLAND in his writings to indicate what is now the northeastern section of the United States. From that noun came a 1632 adjective used in Massachusetts: " 'Tis a ridle as yet to me whether you meane any Elder in these NEW ENGLISH churches." The two-word modifier has not lasted, nor has the Latin phrase for New England, NOVA ANGLIA.

The Latin phrase, which is now obsolete in English, was eventually combined into a single word to indicate the inhabitants of the colonized area. By 1752, this noun was used in an economic study of the New Englanders' overuse of credit: "The NOVANGLIANS in general, the Rhode-Islanders in particular, . . . have hit on the Art of enriching themselves by running in debt." Today's credit-heavy consumers should remember the colonial coinage for late payments, which were derided in 1758 as BEHINDMENTS.

In New England, the Plymouth colony needed a term for the person responsible for keeping order. That officer, who was the town crier as well as the local constable, became known as the MESSENGER, from a Middle English noun related to "message." The Plymouth Laws of 1633 announced, "It is ordered that all measures be brought to the Messenger or Constable of Plym. to be sealed." A decade later, that title was changed to the more familiar "marshal."

Moving about in the new country led to the still-favored phrase PULL UP STAKES. That term, however, did not originate with the tents of western wanderers. Instead, it started in the colonial system of setting stakes to mark the boundaries of a settler's land; a 1640 traveler, reluctant to stay in New England, was quoted as saying, "I am loth to hear of a stay, but am plucking up stakes with as much speed as I may."

The verb in that phrase, whether "pull" or "haul" or "pluck," was eventually deleted, so that "to up stakes" was also a sign of the intention to move. By 1837, a New York resident supported a local law by writing, "If we can't go according to that rule, then I say let every man upstakes and go to Turkey or China." In contrast, finding a place to remain was expressed with "to drive stakes" or "to set stakes."

Of greater concern to settlers was the nearness of their location to town or to one another. A term proved necessary for anybody who chose to live in a remote area. These frontier folk became known by the unlikely term of OUTLIVERS. In

1675, a Connecticut leader recommended in times of danger "that all out livers . . . doe take a speedy and effectuall course to get their women and children . . . to places of the most hopeful security." To the South, an outlying area of development took on a longer term. A Georgia writer in 1740 reported "matters here and there among our OUT-SETTLEMENTS," and its dwellers were known as—what else?—OUT-SETTLERS.

Independence of vocabulation, or "word choice," has been the hallmark of the language since it first began to separate from British English. The spirit of New World independence, however, was never meant to be limited to natives or colonists. As Abraham Lincoln intoned in Philadelphia's Independence Hall in 1861, the Declaration of Independence "gave liberty not alone to the people of this country, but hope to all the world, for all future time."

BLOW BY BLOW

America's words have often shown their independence by stretching their meanings in significantly different directions.

AIRLINE began in 1813 as the term for any straight or direct line, what is now frequently described with the noun "beeline" or the phrase "as the crow flies." By the middle of the nineteenth century, the term was applied to any direct railroad route for "air-line railroad," and since the end of World War I, "airline" indicates a company for air transportation.

Several noun senses have developed from the onomatopoeic word BLOW. In the 1820s, Harvard students used "blow" for a drinking party. In 1851, a hunter in the Rocky Mountains used the term for "scent" or "smell," as in "I did not fire until they came almost within 'blow' of me, and then shot two." A few years later the same noun meant "rest," in giving tired horses a blow, and Harriet Beecher Stowe, in her

1852 novel *Uncle Tom's Cabin,* expressed the question "What's the matter?" by asking "What's the blow now?"

Sometimes a modern usage is more derogatory than the sense it replaces. The clipped form TYPO, for example, now indicates a mistake, short for "typographical error," as in the Washington, D.C., bookstore that offers a shelf of books on "Speling." Back in 1816, however, the same four letters of "typo" stood for "typographer," designating the profession of typesetter.

With other words, however, the newer sense packs less punch than the predecessor. In journalism, for instance, BEAT now refers to any regularly covered area of news, such as the police beat, perhaps from the image of a beaten path. That same noun, however, was applied more than a century ago to what would now be called an "exclusive"; in 1873, *Harper's Magazine* reported, "One of these 'enterprising' individuals secured his first 'beat' by riding in from the first Bull Run defeat on a horse not his own, and taking news of the disaster to Philadelphia by rail, before an injunction was laid on the transmission of the truth." Apparently the earlier journalism meaning came from "beating out" the competition for the first report of a newsworthy event.

In a similar leveling, EXERCISE is now used for healthful physical activity as well as a ceremony such as "graduation exercises." In the early nineteenth century, however, the same word referred to the convulsions caused by excitement during religious revival services. An 1804 *Western Sketch-Book* explained: "The only thing with us which can be construed into disorder or extravagance, is the motions of the body under the exercise. In most of the cases, when the paroxysm begins to go off, the subject feels the strongest desire for prayer."

Humor has also led to the forming of related terms. BASE-BALLER, for instance, was first used in 1867 to indicate anybody who plays or supports the sport of baseball. A humorous homophone, BASE-BAWLER, debuted the same year. The

Chicago Times in July 1867 wrote about "Base-bawlers—the men who, having lost some money in the late match, are asserting that they have been swindled." Over the past two centuries, the officious DOCTOR has been applied to everything from a small engine for supplying a ship's boilers with water to the cook in a logging camp. Similarly, slangsters at the turn of the century turned the dollar bill, known since the Civil War as a GREENBACK from the color of paper money, into a much more graphic coinage: FROGSKIN.

OLD NEWS

Independent thinking has caused the national vocabulary to mushroom, with the new meanings adding to the old ones without replacing them.

In the restored colonial capital of Williamsburg, Virginia, America's old and new words have learned to coexist. Passing through the heart of the historic town, travelers observe the local MAGAZINE on the way to the maker of PERUKES and other shops of the MIDDLING SORT. At the nearby College of William and Mary, a vending machine flashes the message "Please SWIPE," and down the brick-lined street a dusty area contains construction materials that are labeled "suitable for FLASHING." A local hotel promises guests that its rooms are "DOWN AND OUT."

The Williamsburg magazine, not a publication of articles and advertisements, is instead the guarded building that once held the colonists' gunpowder and ammunition. That noun came into British English by way of French from the Arabic *makhzan,* meaning "storehouse"; its modern spelling appeared by 1599, and it was during the eighteenth century that the word gained the sense of a publication or periodical containing a storehouse of information. The older "peruke" meant "head of hair" in the sixteenth century, and it was borrowed from an Italian term for "wig," the specialty of the colonial maker of perukes. Small colonial businesses were run by the middling sort, a forerunner of the more familiar 1766 term "middle class."

Among the modern terms found in Williamsburg, the verb "swipe" has redeemed itself. Originally an 1825 verb for a sweeping motion, "swipe" fell into disreputable senses later in the nineteenth century. By 1889, the verb meant "to steal or pilfer" in American English; that low sense, according to the *Barnhart Dictionary of Etymology,* was "originally said to be theatrical slang, in reference to the practice of performers stealing jokes or appropriating stage routines from one another." With the advent of vending machines capable of reading credit cards, however, "swipe" has regained its first sense, inviting the card user to sweep a card along the track for interpreting by the machine.

Similarly, "flashing" suggests a twentieth-century sense of male exhibitionism probably not intended by the construction crew; since 1742, "flashing" has been a noun for "waterproofing material," such as sheet metal used over the angle between a roof and a chimney. The phrase "down and out," used since 1901 to suggest either "impoverished" or "weakened," now describes hotel rooms that are conveniently located "down" (on the first floor) and "out" (on the outside near parking).

Also surprising is the recent headline in a Virginia newspaper that announced, "Shocking Wheat Brings Back Memories." This sense of SHOCKING, unlike the 1703 adjective for "extremely distressing," comes from a fifteenth-century verb for collecting sheaves of grain or stalks of corn into "shocks." The prepared wheat may eventually be used in making DROP BISCUITS, with "drop" used for dropping the dough instead of rolling and cutting it evenly, or in LONGJOHNS, a lengthy doughnut given the same name as the World War II designation of men's long underwear. Perhaps hardest to swallow is the noun MOON, first used in print by Mark Twain in *Life on the Mississippi* to refer to a large round biscuit.

THE STARTING LINE

In America, today's tourists visit historic firsts not only in Virginia but also in other colonial sites, from the witch house on Essex Street in Salem, Massachusetts, to the oldest wooden schoolhouse in St. Augustine, Florida. In Williamsburg, though, visitors have the opportunity when they leave the Governor's Palace to pass beside a vacant lot on which a small plaque is displayed. The plaque commemorates the location of the earliest theater in America, and even though the building was destroyed long ago, its location retains the feeling of "first." In that same colonial town premiered the first professional Shakespeare production in America, with a 1752 performance of *The Merchant of Venice*.

Mixing old and new, the American language is similarly filled with firsts, including the original use of the phrase FIRST LADY. The longer phrase FIRST LADY IN (or OF) THE LAND appeared in 1834 in reference to a prominent woman; "first lady" itself was popularized about 1870 by a journalist reporting on Mrs. Ulysses S. Grant. The alliterative FIRST FAMILY followed for the president's wife and children, and by the 1980s the wife of the vice president took the title of SECOND LADY.

Today the American dialect continues to grow with a fiercely independent spirit. As quickly as new meanings need to be expressed, new terms seem to be instantly invented. Another "first," for instance, will undoubtedly be forthcoming when a new phrase becomes necessary to refer to the husband of the nation's first female president.

First Up

FIRST GOER the term for any early settler, used in Boston as early as 1654

FIRST SHOT an 1840 New Orleans term for especially strong whiskey

FIRST SWATHE a synonym for "first-rate," used since the middle of the nineteenth century

FIRST BEST a Civil War phrase for "top" or "foremost," as in "finished first best in the contest"

FIRST COMER the same as "first goer," but dating back only to the Civil War era

FIRST, LAST, AND ALL THE TIME a political phrase dating back a century to describe support for a candidate that will be permanent or unwavering

FIRST MONEY the top prize in a contest, used before the turn of the twentieth century in Vermont horseracing

FIRST PAPERS since the turn of the century, a term for the first official papers in naturalizing a foreigner

FIRST OF MAY a carnival term dating back to the 1920s for any amateur or newcomer

FIRST-CABIN a twentieth-century nautical term meaning "first-class" or "in the finest fashion"

CHAPTER 2

PRACTICALITY

Soon after drafting the Declaration of Independence, Thomas Jefferson recognized the practical side of the American character in developing a national language. "The new circumstances under which we are placed," Jefferson wrote, "call for new words, new phrases, and for the transfer of old words to new objects." Jefferson's own sense of practicality led him to an inevitable conclusion: "An American dialect will, therefore, be formed."

A generation later, the lexicographer Noah Webster was even more definitive. "In fifty years from this time," Webster commented, "the American-English will be spoken by more people than all the other dialects of the language."

The American dialect has long depended upon the practicality of its users. Our language has grown by borrowing native Americanisms as well as by adapting imported Briticisms; in addition, other references have demonstrated how Americans have incorporated terms not only from British English but also from almost every other known language. Through a ready resourcefulness that blended practicality with independence, our language has been able to expand through the rapid development of a truly American vocabulary.

RATS!

As Jefferson pointed out, the history of the American language has often required the practical application of old words to new situations, resulting in new meanings.

In an 1813 letter, Jefferson registered his disappointment that "the Edinburgh Reviewers, the ablest critics of the age, set their faces against the introduction of new words into the English language; they are particularly apprehensive that the writers of the United States will adulterate it." He attacked that fear of "neologism," a noun that had itself entered the language only in 1800, with ferocity: "Certainly so great growing a population, spread over such an extent of country, with such a variety of climates, of productions, of arts, must enlarge their language, to make it answer its purpose of expressing all ideas, the new as well as the old."

Among these appropriated words are several terms with meanings added or altered in the cause of expressing new ideas. Sometimes, though, that newness has led to the possibility of misunderstanding. Citizens band radio operators in Georgia, for example, may hear reports of "a twenty-foot GATOR lying on the highway" and not realize that the clipped form of "alligator," far from meaning the familiar reptile, is the slang of truck drivers for any long section of retread tire. (Since 1911, ALLIGATORING has also been a term used by painters to indicate the cracking of paint or varnish caused by contraction.)

A similar misunderstanding occurred recently in California, where a union picket sign outside a hospital announced, "This medical facility is full of RATS." An appeals court banned the banner for displaying deceptive language, because the public may fear vermin infestation and not recognize "rat" as a term from labor slang for any contractor who fails to pay prevailing wages. That same slang term has been found in designations of Frank Sinatra and his show-business friends as "the rat pack," as well as in "the rat line" for freshman recruits at the Virginia Military Institute, and for more than a century "rats!" has been an interjection to express disgust or disappointment.

HOOKER has also had more than its share of meanings, from a cow that attacks using its horns to the Florida sponge fisherman who thrusts a hook through sponges. As a term for a prostitute, the noun long predates the Civil War, although its etymology is sometimes wrongly given as the term for any woman who followed the camps of General Joseph Hooker in the War Between the States. John Bartlett explained the term in 1859 as "a resident of the Hook, i.e. a strumpet, a sailor's trull. So called from the number of houses of ill-fame frequented by sailors at the Hook (i.e., Corlear's Hook) in the city of New York." More recently, the noun has also been applied to orthodox Mennonites; an 1880 issue of *Harper's Magazine* pointed to the use of buttons (as opposed to hooks) in that religion: "The stricter Mennonites regarded them as a worldly innovation, and, adhering to the use of hooks and eyes, were called 'Hookers,' in distinction from the more lax brethren, who were called 'Buttoners.' "

Such practicality in the recycling of existing words, as well as independence of invention, is part of an American tradition. As Jefferson himself explained in a letter two centuries ago, "I am not scrupulous about words when they are once explained." He had tried neologizing in his 1781 *Notes on the State of Virginia,* noting that "So far the Count de Buffon has carried this new theory of the tendency of nature to belittle her productions on this side the Atlantic."

After being belittled for this coinage of BELITTLE, Jefferson found unexpected linguistic support from a lifelong rival, John Adams. (When Jefferson died at Monticello on the Fourth of

July in 1826, the fiftieth anniversary of the signing of the Declaration of Independence, his final words were reported as
"This is the Fourth?" Adams, who coincidentally died the
same day hundreds of miles away, was worried instead that
"Thomas—Jefferson—still surv—.") A decade before his
death, though, the second president seconded Jefferson's attempts to create an American dialect. Adams signaled his
favor of a homegrown language by saying, "I approve Jefferson's word *belittle* and hope it will be incorporated into American dictionaries."

THE WRONG WORD

Not all Americans applauded their fellow citizens' practical
attempts to rework the language, however, especially whenever the chosen word did not seem to fit.

More than a century ago, Mark Twain wrote a scathing critique of the literary language of James Fenimore Cooper and
provided a detailed list of the errors committed by Cooper in
reaching for approximate words instead of exact words. Here
are a dozen of Cooper's alleged approximations:

verbal	(for)	oral
unsophisticated	(for)	primitive
fact	(for)	conjecture
explain	(for)	determine
mortified	(for)	disappointed
decreasing	(for)	deepening
treacherous	(for)	hostile
rejoined	(for)	remarked
situation	(for)	condition
distrusted	(for)	suspicious
eyes	(for)	sight
counteracting	(for)	opposing

Twain's own obsession with word precision was perhaps most memorably expressed in his insistence that "The difference between the almost-right word & the right word is really a large matter—it's the difference between the lightning bug and the lightning."

Despite Mark Twain's strictures, the American language has long provided examples of words with multiple meanings. Sometimes the mixing of words and proper names can cause confusion. Reports of a "Bland Music Contest," for example, might elicit little excitement among those who do not know the contest is held in memory of James A. Bland, the African-American composer (and the first black examiner in the U.S. Patent Office) whose works include "Carry Me Back to Old Virginny."

Similarly, a Virginia newspaper reports the naming of "a Batman Road," along with an explanation that "it has nothing to do with the legendary caped crusader; it's drawn from the Batman family that has long lived in the area."

PRACTICALLY SPEAKING

The practicality of reusing old words dates back to the early days of the colonies, and in the centuries since then, multiple meanings continue to persist. A prison official today, for instance, is a WARDEN. In 1662, the town of Providence in Rhode Island used that noun, based on British usage, for an officer akin to a justice of the peace.

TRUCK, before becoming the familiar motor vehicle, also had more than one sense. Before the American Revolution, it took on a meaning of "medicine" in certain localities; a glossary of that period includes a patient's comment that "Till now ne'er crazy, in my bones no pains, I never took no truck, nor doctor's means." By the next century, it referred to vegetables or garden produce, a sense still heard in the western phrase "truck and trade." That sense of bartering grew out of the older English phrase "to have no truck with," which dates back to Shakespeare's time.

PICKUP, a thoroughly American term now associated with motorized trucks, was reported by John Bartlett in his 1848 dictionary of Americanisms: "A pick-up, or a pick-up dinner, is a dinner made up of such fragments of cold meats as remain from former meals." Bartlett added, "The word is common in the Northern States." That term, though, has been largely replaced by "leftovers."

Tampering with a jury became known as WATERING at the end of the eighteenth century. Now obsolete, this term was used in New Hampshire, where one historian noted that "The practice of watering the jury was familiarly known to those persons who had business in the Law." More threatening is the harmless-sounding BELL, used since Revolutionary days for the rattles of any rattlesnake. A 1781 history of Connecticut warns about that type of snake: "Before they bite, they rattle their bells three or four times."

During the nineteenth century, the use of nouns with multiple meanings expanded rapidly. For instance, the African-American orator Sojourner Truth raised money by selling her SHADOW, which was then the term for a photographic likeness. In New England, the noun BARBER was applied to a bitterly cold wind filled with ice crystals that felt as if it were cutting the skin. And even before RECESS took on the sense of "a school break or playtime" in the later part of the century, the noun was used in New York and Ohio as another term for a restaurant or eating place. An 1891 recollection from Buffalo indicates that "The town had an abundance of Restaurants, Recesses and Coffee Houses, as they were variously called."

Verbs often held more than one sense as well. The deadly DECAPITATE became a political term in the middle of the nineteenth century with a sense of "to remove from office." In 1850, Nathaniel Hawthorne headlined a section of his novel

The Scarlet Letter with "The Posthumous Papers of a De-capitated Surveyor," and a political lexicographer explained in 1871 that "When the poor office-holder . . . is superseded by a successor, he is, in political language, beheaded or de-capitated." The related CAPITATION refers to the modern medical practice of HMOs that pay doctors a certain amount per patient, or by the head.

Now applied mainly to music, the verb ROCK was used in Philadelphia in the 1830s for "to throw stones at," and the phrase ROCK OUT began as a westernism three decades later for the process of separating gold from gravel. SALT took on a slang sense of "to kill or do away with"; a spicy 1840 novel in-cludes this usage in "This agent of his excellency . . . once fairly salted, . . . we shall have no trouble for some time to come." (Trickery, however, took on the longer expression SALT THE COW, meaning "to win by indirect methods." Davy Crockett's 1834 autobiography included this folk wisdom: "I went on the old saying, of salting the cow to catch the calf.")

Also growing in meanings were various adjectives. The modifier BAREFOOT began in the early eighteenth century with a variant term, BARE-LEGGED, which also meant "pure" or "uncontaminated"; a journal entry in 1704 noted that "the pumpkin and Indian mixt bred had such an aspect, and the bare-legg'd punch so awkerd or rather awfull a sound, that we left both." The term "barefoot whiskey" prevailed in Ten-nessee for undiluted alcohol, and the adjective was also ap-plied to other forms of drink, as in an 1866 report: " 'I take my tea barfoot,' said a backwoodsman when asked if he would have cream and sugar."

Words that shifted from one part of speech to another have flourished. As early as the Lewis and Clark expedition, the verb RELAX became a noun for intestinal flu, with a report noting "Several of the men Sick with the relax." Nowadays heard more often as an adjective, BALD was used in 1838 as a noun for a treeless mountaintop. A writer for the *Southern*

Literary Messenger that year related, "At length, after considerable fatigue, we came to the top of the near bald; from this we had an extensive and delightful prospect."

Also enriching the American language has been the blending of existing English words, as in the "spoon" and "fork" that merged earlier this century into a SPORK.

Perfect Blends

EXPLATERATE explain + elaborate (an 1831 verb for "to tell or express")

SAVAGEROUS savage + dangerous (an 1832 term for "fierce or wild")

SQUINCH squeeze + pinch (an 1835 blend for "to twist or compress")

SALOONATIC saloon + lunatic (an 1878 word for "bartender or saloon supporter")

TROUSALOONS trousers + pantaloons (a Wild Western humorous term for "pants")

RUCKUS ruction + rumpus (an 1890s mixture for "uproar or noisy commotion")

INSINUENDO insinuation + innuendo (a late-nineteenth-century word for "unfair hinting or suggestiveness")

GREATLE great + while (an early-twentieth-century Long Island term for "long time")

INFANTICIPATE infant + anticipate (a 1930 Walter Winchell coinage for "to expect a baby")

> **TELEPUTER** television + computer (a 1996 noun for "television set connected to the Internet")

ON NATIVE TERMS

Even more practical has been the lifting of language already available in the New World. Many Old American terms came into existence in the relations between the land's natives and the immigrant settlers.

A 1705 visitor to Virginia, who witnessed the activities of the natives in reaching a peaceful agreement, related that "They use . . . very ceremonious ways in concluding of Peace . . . such as BURYING A TOMAHAWK." The name of "tomahawk" was later applied to any hatchetlike tool used by the Indians in the eastern part of the country, and their peaceful saying remains in use, but usually with a variant noun. As a distraught character on a 1997 soap opera announced, "I'm going to make a simple offer to BURY THE HATCHET and start over."

The practice of American Indian warriors in removing the scalps of victims led to the colonists' use of the word SCALPING by 1750. Still current is the phrase "ticket scalping," used since the late nineteenth century. When the British actress Fanny Kemble mentioned this method of selling hard-to-obtain tickets, she wrote in 1833 that "Some of the lower class of purchasers, inspired by the thrifty desire for gain said to be a New England characteristic, sell these tickets, which they buy at the box-office price, at an enormous advance, and smear their clothes with treacle and sugar and other abominations, to secure from the fear of their contact of all decently-clad competitors, freer access to the box-keeper." The practice of scalping or inflating ticket prices, outlawed in many parts of the country, persists despite the legal restrictions.

As natives commingled with the settlers, the English had

the opportunity to observe long-standing customs and activities of those who preceded them. To such activities, an English name would sometimes be given. INDIAN RAZOR, for instance, was the term for a pair of sharp clam shells, which were used to scrape off hair. Eventually the Indians were able to obtain a metal version from traders, and in 1775, an English observer explained, "Holding this Indian razer between their forefinger and thumb, they deplume themselves."

Another English term for a native notion is the phrase GOOSE MOON. It refers to the annual return of the Canadian goose from its southern migration. As an 1850 observer commented, that bird's "arrival in the fur countries, from the south, is impatiently expected; it is the harbinger of spring, and the month is named by the Indians the 'goose moon.'"

Sometimes the native term was not known when an English phrase was substituted. In the South, the annual celebration for the first ears of corn was known in 1725 as the GREEN CORN DANCE. A generation later, the settlers applied the Creek term *paskita,* meaning "feast," to that celebration; the native term was shortened by English speakers to the single word BUSK, described by the anthropologist Sir James George Frazer in 1890:

> Amongst the Creek Indians of North America, the busk or festival of first-fruits was the chief ceremony of the year. It was held in July or August, when the corn was ripe, and marked the end of the old year and the beginning of the new one. Before it took place none of the Indians would eat or even handle any part of the new harvest. . . . Before celebrating the busk, the people provided themselves with new clothes and new household utensils and furniture; they collected their old clothes and rubbish, together with all the remaining grain and other old provisions, cast them together in one common heap, and consumed them with fire.

Made from that crop is what we now call SUCCOTASH, a mixture of corn and beans, which began at Plymouth as a soup. It came from the Narraganset word *misickquatash,* meaning "boiled whole kernels of corn," and was described more than a century ago as "a medley of stewed meat, beans, hominy and peppers." The modern term, which has undergone a number of spelling changes, first appeared in English as "Suckatash" in 1751.

Various spellings have also been given to TOSHENCE, borrowed from the natives of New England. Meaning "youngest child in the family," this noun was not recorded until 1802, when a Massachusetts writer explained: "The Indians of New England had . . . [a] word, which in the dialect of the Nauset Indians was toushents. It has been adopted by descendants of the English in many parts of the Old Colony of Plymouth, and is applied as a term of endearment." Sometimes shortened to TORSH, this noun can still sometimes be heard in the Northeast.

Another term that could be applied to settlers as well as to natives was the descriptive MATCHET. This word for "evil" dates back to 1676 in print, but it received fairly evenhanded usage in a 1705 quotation. "At last," an early report on New England words explained, "he entertained the distinction, that there were matchet Englishmen as well as matchet Indians, . . . matchet, that is to say, naughty or wicked."

WAWA ON WAMPUM

Native customs in early American times led to the practical adoption of many words familiar in modern American usage. A medicine man, for example, was once known by the term POWWOW, which ultimately comes from the Indian term for "he (who) dreams." The term was extended to a loud conjuring ceremony and then to any conference or meeting, a meaning that remains in use. A 1997 advertisement, for instance, of a Virginia celebration by Native Americans was headlined "The Natural Bridge Pow-Wow."

Equally familiar is the term for native money, known as WAMPUM, a shortening of the Algonquian *wampumpeag* for "shell beads on a string." Frederick Hodge explained, "As the native expression was too cumbersome for ready utterance by the New England colonists, the sentence-word was divided by them into wampum, and peak." Governor William Bradford's *History of Plimouth Plantation* included the longer term in a 1627 citation: "Ye above-said parties are to have . . . wampampeak, hatchets, knives, &c." Two centuries later, the idea was Anglicized into the phrase SHELL MONEY. The color of that shell money proved significant, with the term MOWHACKEES applied by natives to dark-colored shells, approximately double the value of white wampum.

Among the most widely recognized of native terms is the tentlike abode known as a WIGWAM. Taken from the Eastern Abenaki term for "dwelling," this word dates back to the colonial days in Massachusetts to denote the death of a native. "When any dies," an English writer noted in 1628, "they say Tanto carries them to his wigwam, that is his house." By the time of an 1845 census, the term was applied broadly to an Indian family: "The Cree nation is considered very powerful, and numbers more than six hundred wigwams."

Not all Indian-based words have direct connection to Native Americans. The name of a subtribe of the Algonquians remains familiar in a term of formal dress. Since 1889, a man's formal attire has been called a TUXEDO. That name was taken from a country club at Tuxedo Park, New York, where the outfit was first worn. Known since the 1920s by the clipped term TUX, this suit bears no other connection to the Indian name.

Another term that is Algonquian in origin and more directly related to Native Americans is the noun RACCOON. It probably comes from the Virginian term *arakun,* meaning "scraper," perhaps referring to the animal's habit of scraping alongside water for crabs to eat. John Smith recorded the term in a 1608 journal entry that the leader Powhatan "each weeke once or twice, sent me many presents of Deare, bread, Raugroughcuns." The term was later applied during the Revolutionary War to any member of the New Jersey militia; a 1779 report ordered "each devoted racoon to receive down forty soft or paper dollars."

A more poetic native term is POTLATCH, from a Chinook word for "gift." By the nineteenth century, this term was being used as a noun for a ceremony of exchanging gifts, as well as a verb for "to give or present." This freedom of giving, however, took on the onus of fines or taxation by the turn of the century; in 1898, a California publication editorialized that "In case the sentence is carried out, they will be compelled to 'potlatch' a very large amount." Also from Chinook is TUM-TUM. This reduplication replicates the beating of the heart and is defined as "heart and mind." An Idaho newspaper printed the term in 1876 to explain the coming of spring: "To describe the really delightful, warm, sunshiny weather . . . would create envious feeling in the tum-tums."

In the Chinook jargon out of the Northwest, the overall term for language and speech is the reduplication WAWA. This term may be used as a verb for "to speak" or as a noun for "speaking." The more general sense of "talk or discussion" appeared in an 1868 account of bargaining with a local tribe by a traveler bound for Alaska: "After a 'hyas wa-wa' (big talk) with the Indians, Brown at length succeeded in hiring a canoe."

Another important early American term is SACHEM, the title of a leader taken from the Algonquian word for "chief." A 1622 journal on the Plimouth Plantation offered this entry: "They brought us to their Sachim . . . very personable, gentle, courteous, and fayre conditioned." Within another century, the word was applied to any political leader, and any area governed by this leader became a "sacherdom" or "sachership."

Early studies of these native words also produced useful information about language formation. "A late grammarian has said that all words were originally monosyllables," Thomas Jefferson observed in an 1825 letter. "The Indian languages disprove this. I should conjecture that the Cherokees, for example, have formed their language not by single words, but by phrases. I have known some children learn to speak, not by a word at a time, but by whole phrases. Thus the Cherokee has no name for 'father' in the abstract, but only as combined with some one of his relations."

Despite its vast growth, even the modern American language has gaps yet to be completed. The coming decade, for instance, is the first of a new century and a new millennium. Unlike the "eighties" and the "nineties," though, no widely acceptable term has been suggested to fill the nameless vacuum for the next ten years.

Pragmatic Americans, however, are undoubtedly up to this linguistic challenge. With practicality an established part of the national personality, America's writers and speakers have always been able to find the ideal term. As Theodore Roosevelt noted almost a century ago, "From the very beginning our people have markedly combined practical capacity for affairs with power of devotion to an ideal."

CHAPTER 3

BOLDNESS

"Since everything goes by steam and electricity," a midwestern writer boasted in 1856, "tall walking and tall talking are the vogue."

Expressing the boldness of the American spirit, talking tall has always been at least as important to the national image as walking tall. The modifier TALL, far more than a simple indication of height, appeared as early as the 1830s in expressions of pride or extravagance. "One of the striking peculiarities of our people," *Knickerbocker Magazine* commented in 1842, "is the disposition to talk tall."

Since the days of the American frontier, tall talk has distinguished the language of a people facing new challenges and opportunities. Frontiersmen like Davy Crockett boasted with new and ever-lengthening words about their abilities to outspeak other pioneers. Often their boasts made claims as exaggerated as their words, but they wanted the rest of the world to recognize the legacy of their land. "If I could rest anywhere," Crockett once opined, "it would be in Arkansaw where the men are of the real half-horse, half-alligator breed such as grows nowhere else on the face of the earth."

FISHING LINES

Often the tall talk was woven with great bravado into a "tall tale." Marjorie Tallman's *Dictionary of American Folklore* defines that type of story as "an exuberant combination of fact with outrageous fiction." It was also mentioned in a 1927 poem, when Stephen Vincent Benét eulogized Abraham Lincoln as "six feet one in his stocking feet, . . . / Whose wit was a coonskin sack of dry, tall tales."

The earlier term was TALL STORY. In Arkansas around 1845, one tall talker recounted that "A 'live Sucker' from Illinois . . . had the daring to say that our Arkansaw friend's stories 'smelt rather tall.' " These stories would be related or, as westerners might say, LET OUT. An 1847 account of a storyteller's art begins, "Tom squared himself for a yarn, wet his lips with a little corn juice, took a small strip of Missouri weed, and let out."

Marjorie Tallman's collection included what she labeled the "tame trout" tale. "In the Ozarks," the folklorist wrote, "they have a popular tale that is offered to gullible visitors. It is about a tame trout. He follows his owner about and really becomes quite a pet. However, in crossing a bridge one day the trout slips off into the brook and is drowned." Exaggerated fishing stories are still popular, particularly in storytelling contests.

On the prairie, the pioneers of the eighteenth and nineteenth centuries also measured the tallness of their tales by the animals inhabiting the stories. Any BEAR STORY, for example, exaggerated the existence or hunting of bears by pioneers. A newspaper account in 1856 weighed the merits of one such tale: "Whether the forty-bear-in-a-day story . . . was founded on fact, or was merely a bear-story, we are unable to decide." A generation earlier, the FISH STORY had entered the language. In a St. Louis newspaper, an 1819 fish story was related wherein "In consequence of the shoals of white-fish which . . . choaked the channel . . . the steamboat could not pass." By 1826, a newspaper in Fredericksburg, Virginia, was recounting a SNAKE STORY, defined by Mitford Mathews as "a tall story in the manner of a bear or fish story." This type of tall tale led to another phrase, TO FALL A SNAKE, for use by those skeptical of the exaggerations. In an 1820 letter from the West, one man said of snakes, "I killed a hundred of them . . . in a few minutes, each as large as my leg." The skeptic who heard the claim replied, "I do not dispute it . . . but would be better satisfied if you would fall a snake or two."

Sports fans will note that these tall tales have also given rise to fictitious accounts of their favorite games. A 1912 base-ball report, for example, mentions that from the South "drift tales each spring of . . . the 'stop ball.' " This tall term refers to a pitched ball that, just before reaching the batter, suppos-edly comes to a dead stop.

This century's equivalent to the tall tale is known as the URBAN LEGEND, primarily spread by speech or print. Rarely involving the wild words of tall talk, these legends feature un-corroborated stories of alligators found in city sewers or Mex-ican rats mistaken by Americans for small dogs. Even more recent is the E-MAIL HOAX, ranging from premature reports of celebrity deaths to a recent find of a prehistoric skull in New Jersey (the skull, it turned out, came from a Barbie doll).

Tall Talk

GALLINIPPERS large mosquitoes or stinging insects (a 1634 noun of uncertain origin, possibly from insects that infest a ship's kitchen, or "galley")

ABSQUATULATION fast departure or escape (a fanciful nineteenth-century term perhaps based on "abscond")

OBFLISTICATED bewildered or overcome (a nineteenth-century humorous variation of the verb "obfuscate")

RIPSNIPTIOUS smart or particular (an 1830 southern and western term sometimes clipped to "sniptious")

RANTANCKEROUS quarrelsome or stubborn (an 1832 adjective apparently blending "rancorous" and "cantankerous," and leading to the noun "rantankerosity")

SOGDOLLAGER somebody exceptional or unusual (an 1838 variation of "sockdolager," perhaps based on "sock" for a punch and "doxology")

POKERISHNESS unearthliness (the 1845 noun based on the 1827 adjective "pokerish" for "having a ghostly or dreadful appearance")

GALLEY-WEST unconscious (an 1875 Mark Twain usage—perhaps based on the English dialect term "colly-west"—used in "to knock galley-west")

RANTUM-SCOOTUM scattered or disorderly (a rare 1885 variation of the rhyming expression "rantum-scantum," similar to "harum-skarum")

EVENTUALIZE to come to pass (a turn-of-the-century verb form of the adjective "eventual")

STRETCH MARKS

In the bold telling of the earlier tales, appropriately exaggerated language became necessary for enhancing the overstated details. Many of those words, shaped and stretched from existing terms, make up the tall talk that enlivened life on the prairie and all points east and west. Whenever the older words of English seemed inadequate, Americans boldly and brazenly extended the existing terms, particularly with the added syllables of tall talk.

The quality of letting such a story go at full pace was known by the unwieldy noun LET-HER-RIP-ITIVENESS. In 1857, a San Francisco observer of a new business "decided that there was a good deal of honesty of purpose hid under an assumed appearance of let-her-rip-itiveness." A similarly stretched term is a synonym for "perseverance," STICK-TO-IT-IVENESS; it was first used in an 1867 story about "Old Rover, with the stick-to-it-iveness of a fox-hound when once on a trail." Thomas Edison picked up the term, and that inventor's advice about creativity is still featured in a display at Disneyland: "The three great elements to achieve anything worthwhile are, first, hard work; second, stick-to-it-iveness; third, common sense."

The extension of America's vocabulary was often built on existing British words. The verb "bulge," for instance, appeared in British English as a variant of "bilge" in the fifteenth century. Americans took that term for "to swell or enlarge" and turned it into the noun BULGER to indicate anything large. In 1835, Davy Crockett used the term to comment when he "came in sight of the great city of New York, and a bulger of a place it is." Lawyers extended the language with SUABILITY, defined by Noah Webster as "Liability to be sued; the state of being subject by law to a civil process." John Jay, the first Chief Justice of the Supreme Court, introduced the term in a 1793 letter: "The second object of inquiry now presents itself, viz., whether suability is compatible with State sovereignty." The verb "sue" appeared back in Middle English, and the adjective form "suable" was also a British borrowing, which dates from Shakespeare's time.

Sometimes the adding of a suffix to an existing word provided a new way to express a meaning. By ending the noun "hornet" with another letter, Americans were able to express "extremely angry" with the adjective HORNETY; an 1834 letter described a military leader with this expression for an emotion beyond anger: "The Gineral got as hornety as all nature at this." An adjective like ORNERY, which was probably a variant of "ordinary," took on a suffix for the noun form, ORNERINESS. By the end of the nineteenth century, the American novelist Booth Tarkington used the expression to indicate meanness: "Sometimes they . . . let loose their deviltries just for pure orneriness." In Georgia, the central syllable of "opinionated" was altered to creat the term OPINUATED, meaning "conceited," and in 1781 the Reverend John Witherspoon referred to a syllable added to "confiscate" for CONFISTICATE, which he pointed out as a saying of "the most ignorant of the vulgar." Occasionally, though, the addition came at the start of the term, as in the formation of the adverb SEMI-OCCASIONALLY, used in 1854 to describe a minister who "preached semi-occasionally, at a private house."

Noise that was not necessarily talk was known as CLATTERWHACKING since the middle of the nineteenth century. The rattling sound built from the shorter "clatter" led Mark Twain to CLATTERY, an 1880 adjective. Twain used the term to write of "a small piano in this room, a clattery, wheezy, asthmatic thing."

Even a word as simple as "oldest" could be stretched by the tall talkers. Western speakers turned that superlative adjective into the longer OLDERMOST. It first appeared in 1843 and was repeated in print a decade later in a western tale:

" 'Where is your oldermost child?' said the man to the unfortunate father."

Other bold entries were fanciful formations, such as the slang verb HORNSWOGGLE. That term for "to bamboozle or cheat" dates back to 1829, when it was identified as a Kentucky expression for "to cause embarrassment." (BAMBOOZLE, more than a century older, is of unknown origin.) As recently as 1948, however, *The Chicago Tribune* still used the term, in an article about a farmer who "came into the Central police station and reported he was hornswoggled out of $180." The word would inevitably be stretched, and an even longer noun form of the verb appeared after the Civil War: HORNSWOGGLEMENT.

The stretching of words is still heard in everyday conversation. The word CONVERSE, for instance, may be extended by inserting an extra syllable. Reporting a recent power outage, *The Washington Post* interviewed urban families about life without television, and one woman responded, "You can sit and CONVERSATE more than you would." Even more controversial is ETHNICATE, used since the early 1990s for the business practice of trying to separate customers into racial or ethnic categories.

MYTH INFORMATION

Amid the boldness of tall talk, some of the fanciful American formations may have been influenced by existing terms for mythical creatures.

CATAWAMPUS, for instance, has long been fiercely debated as a word of various origins. It is recorded as early as 1833 as the term for a remarkable or odd creature, jocularly applied to a person. Also suggested as a mythical creature of the Southwest, this noun may have come from "catamount," another term for "wildcat." At the same time, however, "catawampus" has been used in other parts of the country for "askew, out of alignment."

That sense may have been influenced by the 1838 modifier "catercorner," heard in dialect as "catty-corner" or "kitty-corner," to indicate a position diagonally opposed to the user. As *National Geographic* reported in a 1931 issue, "A new fence post, set out of line, is 'catawampus.'" (Other off-center synonyms include SLANTENDICULAR, a blend of "slant" and "perpendicular," and the fanciful New England term OB-SCUTELY.) Various meanings for the term "catawampus" may have conflated as early as this report in an 1839 New Orleans newspaper: "Things have been goin' on in a catawompussed fix for a long time, nary party ownin' the land yet both makin' jest as free as though they had it reg'larly deeded over to 'em."

SNOLLYGOSTER is another tall term of various backgrounds and meanings. Defined in the unabridged *Random House Webster's Dictionary of the English Language* as "a clever, unscrupulous person," this noun dates back to just before the Civil War. In 1895, the *Columbia Dispatch* reported, "A Georgia editor kindly explains that 'a snollygoster is a fellow who wants office, regardless of party, platform or principles, and who, whenever he wins, gets there by the sheer force of monumental talknophical assumnacy.'" (Anybody using that last phrase today would be called simply a "fast talker.")

William Safire, in his dictionary of political terms, defined the term as "an unprincipled politician; according to Harry Truman, 'a man born out of wedlock'"; the columnist tracked Truman's revival of the term to a 1952 speech in West Virginia, as a put-down of politicians who use public prayer to win votes. In Maryland, the variant spelling is SNALLY-GASTER, perhaps derived from the German *schnelle geister,* meaning "wild ghost." *Merriam-Webster's Third New International* defined that variant word a generation ago as "a mythical nocturnal creature that is reported chiefly from rural

Maryland, is reputed to be part reptile and part bird, and is said to prey on poultry and children."

The ability to fight mythical creatures required equally mythical language, such as the fanciful CONBOBBERATION. The 1835 term for "fuss or disturbance" was popularized by an 1845 fish story. That tale was of a major battle in landing a giant fish: "There was somethin' a flouncin' and sloshin', and makin' a devil of a conbobberation at the end of the line." Also of unknown origin is SQUMPTION, which means "speed" or "hurry": "Hold on, fellers," an 1854 story advised, "don't be in such a squmption." The hero of a tall tale who acts "uppity" or above others was guilty of GOSTRATION. In an 1840 edition of *The Congressional Globe,* a fierce fighter was exaggerated as having "the blustering gostration of the cock" that would allow him to "scare the enemy to death without a fight and save his powder."

TAFFY TERMS

The boldest coinages of tall talking frequently took on more than one spelling or form. The verb EXFLUNCT was used since 1831 to mean "to use up or overcome completely." Within another decade, the verb had been enlarged to EXFLUNCTICATE in a New York newspaper and stretched to EXFLUNCTIFY in the nation's capital. Both of the longer forms have survived into this century, including the use of "exflunctified" in 1969 to indicate that somebody was inebriated.

For emboldened Americans, a single word could offer far different connotations. BANKMAN, for example, began in 1834 as a political term for any supporter of the United States Bank. The same term, however, appeared after the turn of the century as the label for a bank robber. A 1901 survey of criminal activity across the country asked, "Do you think Boston is as much of a bank-man's hang-out as it used to be?"

SLUMGULLION, a term from mining for the mud dredged out of streams, was identified in 1879 as a western term for tea and in 1942 as a midwestern word for bread pudding. Between those uses, the word also was applied to a stew of meat, potatoes, and onions. As early as 1851, Herman Melville reported a variant of this word among the whaling terms in *Moby-Dick:* "It is called slobgollion; an appellation original with the whalemen. . . . It is an ineffably oozy, stringy affair, most frequently found in the tubs of sperm, after a prolonged squeezing, and subsequent decanting."

Among frontiersmen, the thrill of the hunt could produce a condition known as PEEDOODLES for no apparent reason. The more common term for that condition was BUCK FEVER or BUCK AGUE, defined as "the excited case of nerves experienced when a hunter sights a large deer." (F. Scott Fitzgerald complained of sentence fever.) Other animals inspired similar feelings; a visitor to the Midwest commented in 1844, "I have often heard backwoodsmen speak of the 'buck ague,' but commend me to the 'buffalo fever' of the Prairies for novelty and amusement." Similar to the formation of "peedoodles" is the noun SCADOODLES. That word, still heard as a slang term for "large amount," was reported to be in use by 1869: "A Texan never has a great quantity of any thing, but he has 'scads' of it, or 'oodles,' or 'dead oodles,' or 'scadoodles.' "

Terms for those who engaged in tall talk included JAWCRACKER and JAWSMITH. The latter term, which appeared in a St. Louis newspaper in 1886, was defined by the *Century Dictionary* as "One who works with his jaw; especially, a loudmouthed demagogue: originally applied to an official 'orator' or 'instructor' of the Knights of Labor." A more fanciful term for the garrulous was the noun QUATTLEBUM. Anybody overcome or dumbfounded by negative talkativeness was DUMBFOOZLED, an 1845 term that led to the 1888 variant DUMBFLUSTERED.

WAYBACK WORDS

Users of these stretch terms, when not being celebrated for their boldness of language, found themselves derogated as "backwoodsmen" or "waybacks from wayback." A backwoods character, who was celebrated by Mark Twain in an 1889 novel, took the name of "old Grayback from Wayback." WAYBACK itself, originally referring to a distance "way back in the woods," has been updated in the twentieth century to indicate "belonging to a former time." A 1923 history of the frontier stated, "This occurred 'way back,' when the Indians had no horses." The television cartoon series *The Adventures of Rocky and Bullwinkle* featured a time-travel device known as the "Wayback Machine," and in 1997 the CBS network offered weekly movies based on old television shows during a series advertised as "Way Back" Wednesdays.

The first sense of "wayback," however, pointed to the backwoods or a considerable distance from civilized society. *The Boston Globe* in 1884 reported of such a frontiersman that "His unkempt hair, gawky appearance, and homespun suit . . . all bespoke the citizen from wayback." That term was predated by "a way back" or "away back," as in an 1818 journal of an American traveler: "One of the passengers informed me, 'farms and settlements were thicker a way back, where the land was higher.' "

Some western expressions and wayback terms have been used for adding a regional flavor to advertising. "You don't get a craving for this breakfast," the International House of Pancakes announces. "You get a hankerin'. Because even city folks get a hankerin' every now and then." Similarly, a television commercial for the pain reliever Aleve features the mother of a rancher, whose aches Aleve "helped more than you can fathom." (Both HANKER and FATHOM, which date back to before the turn of the century, come from British English, but the terms are widely considered familiar examples of western dialogue.)

Today's favorite phrase for tall talking is THE WHOLE NINE YARDS, although its origin remains a matter of linguistic controversy. Literally dozens of etymologies have been suggested—yardage in football; material to make a suit of clothes, a kilt, or a bride's veil; cubic yards of concrete in a cement truck; length of a machine-gun belt in fighter planes; number of yards (spars) on a sailing ship—most of which are provably wrong, and more of which are created all the time. Nobody has yet found the definitive source of "the whole nine yards."

Modern usage may go the whole nine yards in welcoming lengthy words and phrases, but originally the adjective LENGTHY was disdained as an early Americanism. In 1689, a writer contemplated the possibility of keeping the peace in Massachusetts: "I very much fear a dreadfull, lengthy, wasting Indian war." By 1816, Samuel Pickering wrote of the adjective's limited popularity in noting that "This word . . . is applied by us, as Mr. Webster justly observes, chiefly to writings or discourses. Thus we say, a lengthy pamphlet, a lengthy sermon."

Nowadays, though, "lengthy" raises few eyebrows. In fact, it provokes almost no reaction that it is unusual or exceptional, suggesting the lasting usefulness of this bold Americanism.

CHAPTER 4

ORNERINESS

*W*hen Eleanor Roosevelt died at the age of seventy-eight in 1962, her most moving tribute came in a eulogy by the politician Adlai Stevenson. "She would rather light candles," he said of the former first lady, "than curse the darkness."

Cursing, however, has long been part of the American spirit, a potent part that proves itself to be more irascible than admirable. Too much boldness in the American spirit has sometimes led to aggression, expressing itself in curses, insults, and swearing as well as fighting. The development of what is called "bad" language reflects a darker side of the American character, specifically a national orneriness.

Insults and invective have long infiltrated the American language. Intended or not, regional slurs tend to reinforce humor or stereotypes about the various parts of a large and diverse country.

The South, for instance, is often derogated for grammatical idiosyncrasies, and even unintentional lapses can cause laughter. "It has been wet in central New England and from the southern Appalachians to the southern Plains," *The New*

York Times reported the spring weather with unintended humor. "The Southeast has done been dry."

Fighting Words

RISE AT A FEATHER a phrase meaning "to become angered easily," used by Thomas Jefferson in 1794 to complain about "being so patient of the kicks and scoffs of our enemies, and rising at a feather against our friends"

WAR TRAIL James Fenimore Cooper's 1840 phrase from American Indians as a variant of the 1755 "war path"

BEECHER'S BIBLES an 1850s term, now historical, for Sharps rifles bought for Kansas antislavery emigrants and funded by the clergyman Henry Ward Beecher

FREE FIGHT a large-scale, riotous brawl, used in Kentucky before the Civil War as a forerunner of the 1881 term "free-for-all!"

REBEL YELL the Civil War term for the typical yell of southern soldiers when going into action on the battlefield

GET ONE'S MAD UP a phrase in use after the Civil War for becoming very angry or "fighting mad"

KEEP A PRIVATE GRAVEYARD an 1880s phrase recorded by Mark Twain and explained in an 1888 slang dictionary: "men who affect great ferocity, or who assume to be desperadoes, sometimes boast in America that they keep graveyards of their own in which to bury their victims"

BRING ON YOUR BEARS an 1880s challenge for an opponent to "do your worst" or "take your best shot"

CRAWL OUT a disparaging turn-of-the-century noun for a backdown or retreat from a fight

FINISH FIGHT an alliterative 1909 term for all-out combat, from a shortening of the phrase "fight to the finish"

NORTH AND SOUTH

The growth of the nation spawned a growth in regional English, which has long been an interest of America's word watchers, but the local labels that Americans have developed for neighboring regions have not always been complimentary.

In the earliest version of the dictionary by Noah Webster, the problems posed in explaining simple directions became apparent: he defined "north" and "south" only as opposite directions, with "east" and "west" identified in relation to the rising and setting of the sun. Webster's 1806 edition also contained the proper abbreviations for the seventeen existing states at that time, as well as the district of Maine and the territories of Indiana and "Missisippi" (which he spelled without its fourth *s*).

Regional variation in language is nothing new, but preferential treatment was definitely given to New England's words two centuries ago in the movement of that language. In an introduction to that first American dictionary, Noah Webster of Massachusetts explained that "provincialisms of New England are more familiar to our ears than those of any other section of the United States, as they are not confined within the limits of those States, but have extended to New York, Ohio, Indiana, Illinois and Michigan; which States have been, to a greater extent, settled by emigrants from New England."

Webster's words were written a generation after the American Revolution had succeeded. In that era, there was a counterbalancing movement toward a national spirit, one meant to overlook regional differences. Probably the most eloquent speaker for that outlook was Patrick Henry, who told the First Continental Congress in 1774, "I am not a Virginian, but an American."

In the century after Patrick Henry, however, regional insults intensified, becoming more the rule than the exception. Words that are no longer current were being used to denote those who lived in other parts of the country. John Russell Bartlett, in his 1848 *Dictionary of Americanisms,* included as an example the entry for SOUTHRON: "A term borrowed from Scotland, and often applied to natives of the South." Today SOUTHERNER is the surviving term, but the other word appeared in a New York newspaper's speculation in 1848 that presidential election lobbying would "prevent the nomination of Gen. Butler, or any other Southron." As early as 1828, a North Carolina politician offered this sentiment: "I am a Republican in principle, and a Southron in feeling." There was never a "Northron," but more than a century ago, a Westerner might be known by the rare title of WESTERNITE. A report on a Pennsylvania election in 1886 noted enviously that "The Westernites are ahead of us."

American writers and politicians have been particularly adept at indicating the differences between regions. "New England is provincial and doesn't know it," Thomas Wolfe commented, "the Middle West is provincial and knows it and is ashamed of it, but God help us, the South is provincial, knows it, and doesn't care."

A specific state, though, could sometimes lead to a poetic insight as well. As the American novelist John Steinbeck once effused, "Texas is a state of mind."

STATING SLURS

"Be Nice to New Jersey" week came just in time. The Associated Press noted the state's salute in 1997, adding that "Poking fun at New Jersey—whether it's jokes about hazardous waste dumps, syringes on the beach or organized crime—is an American tradition." Those put-downs are nothing new in America, symptomatic of the occasional orneriness of the American spirit.

For the 1962 nonfiction book *Travels with Charley,* John Steinbeck toured great extents of the country with his dog and recorded his perceptions of the people along the way. He was warned, however, not to ask directions in Maine from any native of the state. When Steinbeck asked the reason, the response of the Maine resident was telling: "Somehow we think it is funny to misdirect people and we don't smile when we do it, but we laugh inwardly. It is our nature."

Cities could also be the recipients of inventive invective. Mark Twain, for instance, came up with a deft put-down of Los Angeles: "It's a great place to live, but I wouldn't want to visit there." Similarly, after President John F. Kennedy became familiar with the ways of the nation's capital, he was quoted by Arthur M. Schlesinger Jr. on that city. "Washington," Kennedy cleverly remarked, "is a city of southern efficiency and northern charm." Sometimes, though, the put-downs have been unintended. During the 1996 presidential campaign, for instance, a tired Bob Dole was chided by the media for referring to "the Brooklyn Dodgers," a baseball team that had long been relocated to Los Angeles. Dole's slip, however, was at least less laughable than the team's nineteenth-century name might seem: "the Brooklyn Bridegrooms."

Since 1788, PHILADELPHIA LAWYER has indicated an attorney especially hard to outwit, but that term apparently originated in Britain; in that year, a correspondent in London wrote to a Pennsylvania friend, "They have a proverb here, which I do not know how to account for;—in speaking of a difficult point, they say, it would puzzle a Philadelphia lawyer." Almost two centuries later, the lexicographer Mitford Mathews speculated that this term, far more successful here than in the mother country, may have resulted from the legal maneuvers and negotiations abroad by Benjamin Franklin, the Philadelphia statesman, but its basis remains unknown.

Even before the Revolution, different parts of the country have been marked by specific slurs. Benjamin Franklin himself in a 1767 essay mentioned that "There have been . . . Missisippi and South-Sea schemes and Bubbles." MISSISSIPPI BUBBLE was a 1717 financial scheme developed in France with paper money; aimed at trading in on economic opportunities in the Mississippi area, especially Louisiana, this bubble burst and ended disastrously for its investors.

Before Gold Rush Fever caused mass movement to California and then Alaska, the desire to move from one area to another was depicted as "fever," suggesting sickness as well as eagerness. Out of New England, those who sought western expansion were mentioned in an 1832 book about Maine as having "the infatuating spirit of emigration to the Western States—tauntingly denominated the 'OHIO FEVER.'" The urge to move to the Oregon Territory was naturally known as OREGON FEVER, which spread through the Mississippi valley in 1841; in congressional debates about admitting Oregon to the Union back then, senators made vague references to the wild country and the possibility there of cannibalism.

Nobody proved the charges of cannibalism, but the practice of using state names for slurring continues with today's travelers. The GEORGIA BUGGY, for instance, is a wheelbarrow. Drivers recognize the MISSOURI PASS, the daredevil stunt of driving around another car by using the shoulder of a two-lane road. The MISSOURI STOP is a rolling stop, a popular maneuver that has advanced from L.A. STOP and HOLLYWOOD

STOP to ARIZONA STOP and ST. LOUIS STOP; it indicates a slight slowing at a stop sign or red light before proceeding. The KENTUCKY RIGHT TURN is a dodge to the left before making the right turn, and GEORGIA OVERDRIVE is a shift into neutral.

In the early nineteenth century, VIRGINIA WEED was the designation for tobacco. The NEW YORK KISS, although it sounds romantic, refers to a punch in the face. ALABAMA MARBLES are dice, sometimes also referred to as MISSISSIPPI MARBLES. The MISSISSIPPI FLUSH (also subject to many other state names) indicates a hand of any five cards and a revolver. On the other hand, an ARKANSAS FLUSH tries to fool the other players by showing four good cards and keeping the fifth card, which is useless, out of sight.

Financial dealings, often dishonest, have also acquired geographic names. MICHIGAN BANKROLL denominates a large wad of singles with a one-hundred-dollar bill wrapped around the outside to mislead the observer. An OKLAHOMA CREDIT CARD is a length of hose for syphoning gas from somebody else's automobile tank, and a swindle is known less than fondly as a GEORGIA SCUFFLE.

Before being replaced by a national currency, local money could also be devalued by its place name. KANSAS CITY MONEY was subjected to this warning in an 1877 travel guide: "Travelers west should take care how they spend money here in Kansas City, because they have what they call 'Kansas City money,' which is worth only 80 cents on the dollar, and is hard to get rid of, as the people don't care about taking it." BOSTON QUARTER means a nickel, BOSTON DOLLAR a penny. In a Maryland restaurant recently, a diner cunningly asked, "Do you accept HAWAIIAN MONEY here?"

Food and animals have produced many slurs, and sometimes more than one state may be involved in the designation. A ham, for instance, was said to have a MARYLAND END, reported in 1859 to be the hock, with the other side its VIRGINIA END. New York residents have used ALBANY BEEF since 1779 as a jocular term for fish, specifically the sturgeon in the Hudson River. ALASKA TURKEY refers to salmon, and GEORGIA ICE CREAM is a serving of grits. The CAROLINA ROBIN is smoked herring, and the CAROLINA RACEHORSE is a razorback hog. Since the Civil War, a hog has also been called a MIS-SOURI BEAR; *Harper's Magazine* reported in 1866 that "It was quite common for the boys there to go out of nights and kill Missouri bears." The NEW JERSEY EAGLE is a mosquito, and an ARIZONA NIGHTINGALE, like the ROCKY MOUNTAIN CANARY, denotes a braying burro.

Trademarks sometimes become linked with the geographical insult, particularly in American literature. ALABAMA KLEENEX, for example, refers to toilet paper, and writers have also used COLORADO KOOL-AID for beer, originally Coors. The slang of hardboiled detective novels includes NEVADA GAS, used by Raymond Chandler in a mystery to refer to cyanide.

Sometimes the identification is by the name of a city or locale smaller than a state. LAS VEGAS THROAT refers to a husky voice obtained by singing in smoke-filled lounges. A CHICAGO PIANO, like a CHICAGO SEWING MACHINE, is a submachine gun. Since 1829, New Yorkers have used ALBANY BEER for northern cider, and more recently a beer entirely of foam has a CONEY ISLAND HEAD.

Even the newest state has had its name derogated. HAWAI-IAN TIME, also called ALASKA TIME or JAMAICA TIME, refers to inexact time or a lack of punctuality. For the quick passing of time, a NEW YORK MINUTE is a southernism dating back a generation.

Of all the states, however, Arkansas vies with California as the hardest hit by these slurs. An ARKANSAS CHICKEN or T-BONE is bacon, an ARKANSAS WEDDING CAKE cornbread. A chamber pot is termed an ARKANSAS FIRE EXTINGUISHER, and an ARKANSAS TOOTHPICK (sometimes called a CALIFOR-NIA TOOTHPICK) is a sharp weapon like a Bowie knife. The lexicographer John Bartlett reported in 1848 the use of BEAR STATE as the western nickname for Arkansas. When Bartlett asked a Westerner whether the state abounded in bears, the man replied, "Yes, it does; for I never knew a man from that State but he was a bar, and in fact the people are all barish to a degree."

California Calls

CALIFORNIA BIBLE a gambler's deck of playing cards

CALIFORNIA BLANKET a newspaper used for cover by the homeless when sleeping

CALIFORNIA BREAKFAST an orange and a cigarette (sometimes slurred as a "Mexican breakfast," which is a glass of tequila and a cigarette; even older is the "Kentucky breakfast," described in Century Magazine in 1882: "His morning meal was a simple Kentucky breakfast—'three cocktails and a chaw of terbacker' ")

CALIFORNIA DRIVER a motorist who ignores the rules of the road

CALIFORNIA MOCCASINS the use of newspapers by the homeless to wrap their feet

CALIFORNIA OVERSHOES another term, along with "California socks," used for newspaper as foot covering for the homeless

CALIFORNIA PRAYER BOOK another term for "California Bible"

CALIFORNIA STOP the rolling stop of a car at a stop sign

CALIFORNIA SUNSHINE the nickname for a hallucinogenic drug, a type of LSD

CALIFORNIA TIRES tires with no tread left

PLACE PUT-DOWNS

The ornery expressing of regional rivalry is not new to the United States, though it seems to flourish in all parts of the country. Although the TEXAS TWO-STEP indicates a stomach illness, other parts of the world have also been used to name intestinal flu, from the ASIAN to the MEXICAN TWO-STEP. Visitors to Mexico have also called it MONTEZUMA'S REVENGE, and it has been known by those who took ill in India as the rhyming DELHI BELLY, or in Egypt as GYPPY TUMMY.

The practice of deriding place names is at least as old as 1727, when a British book of receipts (or recipes) included an entry for preparing a rabbit in such a way that it would appear and taste like a pheasant. The cookbook added, "This is called, by the topping Poulterers, a Poland-Chicken, or a Portugal-Chicken." (In the United States, a restaurant chain in the 1990s offered TEXAS PHEASANT Tenders on its menu, with the explanation that "chicken tenderloins" is the actual offering.)

In fact, geographical put-downs still flourish worldwide with usages that began in American English. When two airplanes collide in midair, the slang of flight attendants (once known as "stewardesses") calls the crash a FRENCH KISS. Even more macabre is the shorthand that restaurant cooks use for heating food in a microwave: HIROSHIMA, now used as a verb meaning "to cook in a microwave oven," is based on the 1945 bombing of that Japanese city.

Meanwhile, America's English continues to feature ethnic

insults. DUTCH COURAGE indicates false bravado, often based on alcohol consumption, and INDIAN GIVING is a slur against the generosity of aboriginal Americans. In addition, a Florida businessman admits to a gambit that he has used in many deals over the years. "Talk slow," he tells his colleagues, "I'm from Georgia." Many regional slurs in America, though, are disappearing or becoming difficult to trace.

Michigan, the twenty-sixth state, joined the Union in 1837; its name comes from a Native American term meaning "big lake." People who live in Michigan have long used specific hand gestures to indicate their section of the state. Those in the Lower Peninsula use the MICHIGAN MITTEN, or the hand with the palm opened and the thumb pointing east. Those from the Upper Peninsula use the opposite side of the hand with the pointer finger extended. The same state, however, has lent its name to another mysterious gesture, known only as the MICHIGAN HANDSHAKE.

In 1996, the advice columnist Ann Landers answered a letter from a Pittsburgh reader whose boyfriend had taken photographs of her in the nude without her permission. Ann's advice was forthright as usual: "You can do better. . . . Give him a Michigan handshake and tell him to hit the bricks." Everybody knew what she meant by "hit the bricks," a slang synonym of the 1894 "hit the road" for ordering somebody to leave. A few months later, however, Ann Landers advised her readers about the other expression: "At least 5,000 letters have arrived asking, 'What is a Michigan handshake?' It's a firm, no-nonsense grasp that means 'goodbye' and lets the recipient know you really mean it."

Alden Wood, a language columnist who teaches at Simmons College in Boston, pursued the elusive source of that expression, but to little avail. He reported that the advice columnist's editorial assistant responded, "I heard the expression in Michigan some 40 years ago and took it to mean a permanent farewell . . . a very firm goodbye." Folklore experts in Michigan made educated guesses that the state slur was probably from natives of Wisconsin, Illinois, or Ohio. The mystery, however, continues to flourish, and the columnist herself admits that she can do little to settle the question.

"As for that Michigan handshake," Ann Landers now says, "I lived up around Traverse City many, many years ago, and that's where I first heard it. My understanding was that it meant a 'firm, no-nonsense goodbye.'" She admits, though, "The phrase may have passed into disuse because none of my readers wrote to say they'd heard of it."

OH, *!!?!@!

Truth be told, the American spirit has an ornery side that swears by a good oath.

"I confess to some pleasure," Ralph Waldo Emerson admitted in an 1840 journal entry, "from the stinging rhetoric of a rattling oath in the mouth of truckmen and teamsters." To make his point, Emerson added, "How laconic and brisk it is by the side of a page of the *North American Review.*"

Still, the fine art of swearing has not been universally admired in American society. The motion picture code of 1930, for instance, forbade "pointed profanity" and spelled it out parenthetically: "(this includes the words GOD, LORD, JESUS, CHRIST—unless used reverently—HELL, S. O. B., DAMN, GAWD), or every other profane or vulgar expression, however used." Clark Gable's final words in the 1939 film of *Gone With the Wind* exacted a fine for swearing: "Frankly, my dear, I don't give a damn."

Today that line seems tame in comparison to the strong stream of swear words heard on television or in everyday life. In fact, the development of America's language has walked a fine line in its "cursing" (or "cussing"), producing a litany of euphemisms that would allow swearing in what is nowadays rarely called "mixed company."

Perhaps most difficult to determine for our forebears was the problem of swearing without blaspheming. Before the Revolutionary War, both GOSH and GOLLY crossed the Atlantic as euphemisms for "God." A nautical term for sailing by intuition is the twentieth-century BY GUESS AND BY GOD, also known as "by guess and by gosh" as well as "by guess and by golly" and even "by guess and by Godfrey." In 1831, BY GRAVY was added to the list of acceptable curses, and the following decade came BY GUNFLINTS as another mild imprecation.

By 1848, JIMINY CRICKETS was in use as a disguised version of "Jesus Christ," with JIMINY probably by way of GEMINI, and CRICKETS occasionally replaced by CHRISTMAS. The phrase was picked up by Walt Disney for the name of the lovable insect who provided the title character's conscience in his 1940 animated film *Pinocchio*. More popular was GEE, which began numerous expressions of surprise, including GEE WHILLIKIN and GEE WHITAKER in the 1850s. GEE WHIZ, still sometimes heard, began in 1876 as "Gee-wees." Swearing in America has frequently taken on the use of names as euphemisms. Those who replaced "by God" with the euphemism "by George" reached for an even more patriotic variant, BY WASHINGTON; the ornithologist John Jay Audubon, for instance, wrote in his journal in 1827 that "I have powerfully in my mind to give my picture of the 'Trapped Otter' to Mrs. Basil Hall, and, by Washington, I will."

God was also identified by the euphemistic DAD, ranging from DAD-BURN (first in 1829) and DAD-BLASTED to DAD-BLAMED and even DAD-GUM IT. As early as 1834, a Kentucky writer commented, "I'll be dad shamed if it ain't all cowardice." A variant appeared in the *Southern Literary*

Messenger in 1844: "No body better not tell me . . . that I'll sell my vote; or I'll be dad seized if I don't fling a handful o' fingers right in his face." Twenty-five years later, another publication reported another region's variation: "When he wishes to express a peculiarly fierce and inexorable resolve, a Southwesterner [says] . . . 'dad-snatched if you can.' "

Also to be avoided were direct references to hell. HAIL, CO-LUMBIA, the name of a 1798 patriotic song by Joseph Hopkinson, was extended by the middle of the nineteenth century as a term for hell. An Oregon newspaper in 1854 mentioned the disgruntled response by a politician to a published article, particularly "the note in which he says we gave him Hail Columby."

Milder oaths took on the adjective HOLY. A Philadelphia newspaper used a popular form in 1846: "In I went, one leg, but—holy Egypt! out I cum again, howling!" The interjection HOLY MOSES, first found in 1855, was identified in a 1908 issue of *Dialect Notes* as a phrase out of eastern Alabama, more than a decade after the first use of "holy smoke," originally written as "ho-lee smoke!"

TABOO TERMS

Cusswords (itself a dialect version of "curse words") have long thrived in American speech, mixing humor with orneriness.

The Pocahontas County History of West Virginia, for instance, includes an 1855 letter to the postmaster general explaining why the mail could not be delivered through a snowstorm on Cheat Mountain. Here is the letter in its entirety, in which the frustrated mailman stated, "If you knock the gable end out of hell and back it up against Cheat Mountain, and rain fire and brimstone on it for forty days and forty nights, it won't melt the snow enough to get your d____ mail through on time."

As the list of euphemisms grows, however, the number of obscene or indecent words has dwindled. In fact, there are few words still considered taboo in print or broadcasting, and the offense of using them commands a much-reduced penalty. In 1997, for instance, the Federal Communications Commission lowered the fine for an indecent broadcast from $12,500 to $7,000.

In a stronger statement about propriety in the American language, the commissioners of Kleberg County, Texas, voted in the late twentieth century against the use of "hello" because the greeting contains the word "hell." Even though "hello" is etymologically unrelated to "hell," the Texas community replaced that word of welcome and designated a new official term of greeting: "Heaven-o." That replacement for swearing has somehow failed to proliferate.

Orneriness, however, continues to thrive, along with the swear words. At times, in fact, cursing has its usefulness. As the humorist Finley Peter Dunne observed in 1902, "Th' best thing about a little judicyous swearin' is that it keeps th' temper. 'Twas intinded as a compromise between runnin' away an' fightin'."

CHAPTER 5

SOCIABILITY

"*A*n American has no sense of privacy," George Bernard Shaw complained during a 1933 speech in New York. The Irish playwright continued his harangue about the need for privacy, adding that the average American "does not know what it means. There is no such thing in the country."

Valuing publicity over privacy, the American character tends to reveal itself both in action and in language. Perhaps to contrast with the trait of orneriness in the American spirit, a more cheerful characteristic has long endured in the national spirit: a desire to be sociable. For more than two centuries, the phrase MEETING CLOTHES has described the outfits reserved for wearing on special occasions. More familiar is the 1831 phrase SUNDAY-GO-TO-MEETING (later shortened to the even more familiar SUNDAY BEST) for one's finest outfit, intended to impress others.

In the nation's early days, the social setting was often no more than a religious service or a political gathering. But over the centuries the need for sociability drew together the residents of rural and urban areas alike. This trait, in contrast with the urge for independence, has promoted the uniting of the citizens as well as their states.

Friendly words and phrases denoting social celebrations have developed along with the American spirit of friendliness. At times, in fact, that development has been derogated for going too far. "The American has dwindled into an Odd Fellow," complained Henry David Thoreau in 1849, "—one who may be known by the development of his organ of gregariousness." Without that spirit and its attending words, however, the work of building a new country might have proved much more difficult.

PARTY TIME

The American tongue has produced a plethora of words for social activities, particularly party terms. These terms often promoted strenuous work under the guise of socializing.

Much earlier than the modern BUSINESS LUNCH or POWER BREAKFAST, the language introduced other terms for occasions meant to mix work and relaxation. In New England, for example, the expression FISHING TIME has been used for more than three centuries; it dates back to the Massachusetts Bay colony, when a town's entire attention was periodically centered exclusively on fishing. The phrase appears in the records of 1633 as part of a ruling intended to protect fishing stages or huts from errant livestock: "It is ordered, that if any swine shall, in fishing time, come within a quarter of a myle of the stage att Marble Harbour, that they shal be forfected to the owners of the said stage."

Parties that encouraged work took on many names. SHUCKING was used in 1817 for a party arranged to shuck, or remove husks from, ears of corn, while RAISING meant a community working together to build a neighbor's house, not unlike the activity of today's Habitat for Humanity. In the

1850s, a social occasion for neighbors to help erect a barn's frame became known as a BARN RAISING. By 1860, any gathering to pick ripe berries was called a BERRY PARTY. In the nineteenth century, group meetings to make clothes were called SEWING FROLICS, while gatherings to separate cotton from its seeds became known as PICKING COTTON FROLICS.

Working with food also led to new terms. The making and selling of ice cream to raise money led to the ICE CREAM SOCIABLE in 1873; later terms for the same fund-raising occasion included the ICE CREAM SOCIAL and the ICE CREAM SUPPER. Waffles were served in colonial New York at a gathering known as a WAFFLE FROLIC, and young people were especially fond of the TAFFY BAKE, more commonly known as a TAFFY PULL.

Even the act of housecleaning could become a community project. The *Century Dictionary* reported in 1891 a slang use of the word WHANG, earlier a verb meaning "to work with force." In Maine and other parts of New England, the *Century* said, it referred to "a house-cleaning party; a gathering of neighbors to aid one of their number in cleaning house." Far more strenuous was the STONE FROLIC. An 1823 account of celebrations stated: "If a field has to be cleared of stones, they have what is termed a stone frolic. . . . If Indian corn has to be husked, there will be a frolic for that also."

MAIL PARTY, on the other hand, was not a gathering to celebrate on-time delivery. Instead, it was a westernism since the 1850s used to indicate a group of people who travel in a mail coach. A darker humor was evident in the use of HANGING MATCH, a jocular term for a lynching. In 1833, a midwestern newspaper reported the popularity of such a ghoulish attraction: "Even a hanging-match has brought 20 or 30,000 of them together." (Other light terms for this deadly activity were LYNCHING BEE and WHIPPING BEE, part of a long list of social BEES; a 1922 newspaper article revealed the activities of a secret society, including the notice that "Members of this secret organization . . . in the last 18 months in Texas alone have conducted no fewer than 500 tar and feather parties and whipping bees.")

SPECIAL OCCASIONS

Friendlier get-togethers often used the names of farm utensils in their titles. Since the 1840s, HOEDOWN has indicated a lively dance, perhaps based on the movement in hoeing corn and potatoes; such dances were a form of entertainment at a HOEDOWN PARTY, later also shortened to hoedown. Another term for this type of party is RAKE-DOWN; an 1850 report from Iowa stated, "We had a 'rake down' there that evening, Adam White presiding as fiddler." A similar term is SHINDIG; that noun began as an 1850s southernism for "a blow on the shin"; by the 1870s, it referred to any loud party or dance, a slang sense still heard on occasion more than a century afterward.

Weddings have been celebrated boisterously with a type of event variously called a charivari, shivaree, or belling. A variant spelling of the seventeenth-century French borrowing CHARIVARI is the American SHIVAREE, used since 1843 for a loud musical performance, sometimes accompanied by a playful kidnaping, imposed upon a newly married couple.

The similar BELLING was first recorded in a Civil War diary. H. L. Mencken explained in 1948 that "A noisy serenade to a bridal couple is called both a CALLATHUMPIAN and a belling," and the lexicographer Hans Kurath reported a year later that "SERENADE is the usual term among the folk in Eastern New England . . . , TIN-PANNING in Maryland on both sides of the [Chesapeake] Bay." (TIN PAN, slang since the turn of the century for a cheap or tinny piano, gave rise to the name of New York's Tin Pan Alley, for the tinny sound issuing from overused pianos in the offices of music publishers.)

Since the 1880s, STAG PARTY has been applied to gatherings for men only, usually held for a prospective bridegroom. In a recent development, the term has also been applied to parties attended by men and women who go STAG, or without dates. In 1998, the Associated Press quoted a New York City student going dateless to her high school prom (an 1894 shortening of the seventeenth-century "promenade"): "Women are not shy anymore. They can have fun without a guy."

Funerals have also called for socializing, and in gatherings of the century past, the urge to party merged with practicality. Perhaps most practical was the event known as a FALSE BURYING. An 1836 recollection of that type of social occasion explained its rationale: "When a funeral occurs at too great a distance from the city to procure tea," a southern matron recalled that era, ". . . the body is interred, and the friends afterward celebrate . . . a 'false burying,' where religious ceremonies are performed, and refreshments provided." SITTING-UP PARTY is another southernism for a group of friends who would stay up with a corpse on the night before the funeral.

Since the late nineteenth century, servings of food at such get-togethers would often take the form of POTLUCK SUPPERS. Also known as COVERED DISH DINNERS, these casual buffets produce meals by offering food provided by those who attend. Current eating practice at such parties, including the buffets at wedding receptions, has taken the name of GRAZING, animal imagery perhaps devised from earlier references to bars as "watering holes."

The expectation that partygoers would act properly refined led in New Orleans to the gathering known as a BEHAVING PARTY. In 1829, a biographer commented on a couple visiting Louisiana that "They had been at what . . . are very significantly termed 'behaving parties.' In these, . . . the persons present are supposed to be on their good behaviour." Local to Pennsylvania was the TEA-AND-COFFEE SPLASH, used in the late 1800s for rural gatherings where those hot drinks were served. Today the social occasion is usually a TEA—unless it is a political COFFEE being served.

SOCIAL STUDIES

Some American partygoers have made a living out of socializing; others seem to have majored in the subject in college.

Heavy drinkers at saloon parties have been known for more than a century as SITTERS. An Oregon journal commented in 1868 that in the local saloons " 'Sitters,' as they are called, . . . sit about on chairs to sleep off the effects of drink." Also known as LOUNGERS, these heavy drinkers were often without jobs or homes. In 1938, a New York writer commented that "Bowery barkeeps employed homeless men and women as 'sitters' to shiver near the fire on wintry nights and thus evoke the sympathy of cash customers who would treat them to drinks to the great profit of the house."

Younger partygoers have been known in student slang since the nineteenth century as BIRDS. A writer for *Lippincott's Magazine* more than a hundred years ago reported: "There are men in every college, of whom Yale has its full number, denominated in student slang as birds. The birds are firm believers in the old Epicurean theory that everything in life is subservient to pleasure."

The college bird of the last century preceded the emergence two decades ago of an unspecified creature. Following the success of the 1978 film *National Lampoon's Animal House,* fraternity members have demonstrated their "Greek pride" by helping popularize the phrase PARTY ANIMAL. (The ultimate celebrant has been more recently deified as PARTY GOD.)

Such gatherings have not been limited to the most popular students. Those who consider themselves outsiders known as GEEKS came together last year in an Albany, New York, celebration known as "Geek Pride Day." "Geek" itself came into English in the nineteenth century as a dialect term for "fool"; it has been revived since the First World War, taking on the specific derogations of a carnival performer known for biting the heads off live chickens, or, more recently, an overtly intellectual person. That latter sense has led in the last generation to "computer geeks," the brainy types less likely to be invited to parties.

The act of partying itself has also taken on jazzier language. Since the 1920s, JAZZ AROUND has been a slang phrase for "to seek pleasure, to party." That activity, though, has become expressed more recently in rap slang by the verb phrases KICK IT and THROW DOWN.

Major overnight parties have in the past decade taken on the name of RAVES. Such celebrations, often held in warehouses or other unlikely locations, allowed young people an enclosed environment for undisturbed socializing and dancing to rave music. Also popular in recent years is the type of party known as TAILGATING. The verb "tailgate" came into use after World War II for driving too close behind another car; its extended uses now include walking too closely behind other pedestrians as they enter apartment or office buildings with electronic security doors (the tailgater is able to get inside without a proper key or password). Since 1965, the practice of tailgating at sports events or concerts allows a picnic or party in the parking lot, with food and drinks set on the open tailgate of a truck or car.

While social activity has long been given prominence in the language, negative terms have also developed. One who pushes too much for the society of others may be accused of FORTHPUTTING. That 1856 noun, used by the novelist Harriet Beecher Stowe, is a colloquialism for forwardness or objectionable behavior. Stowe wrote of a woman's reaction to two contrasting characters that "Nina was as much annoyed at Clayton's silence, and his quiet, observant reserve, as with

Carson's forth-putting." That term may have been formed on the analogy of another negative term based on an 1828 adjective: OFFPUTTING.

FIDDLE STICKS

American speakers and writers have long fiddled with the language of sociability. British English, though, may have started it with FIT AS A FIDDLE, found in the seventeenth century as a phrase for good health.

From the older "pay the piper" came the colonial term PAY THE FIDDLER, meaning "to suffer the consequences of one's own actions"; a 1787 letter commented, "If people will dance they must pay the fiddler." Retirement or quitting has long been known as TO HANG UP ONE'S FIDDLE. That phrase was in use by 1830, and the American lexicographer John Bartlett (no relation to the Bartlett of *Bartlett's Quotations* fame) explicated its meaning more than a decade later with "When a man loses his temper and ain't cool, he might as well hang up his fiddle."

Fiddlers themselves, however, have not always been treated kindly in the language. Somebody extremely intoxicated may be described with the phrase DRUNK AS A FIDDLER. That insult dates back to the 1840s (an earlier, vulgar version, "drunk as a fiddler's bitch," dates from the 1820s), and was remembered by Mark Twain in the 1884 novel *Huckleberry Finn:* "Toward daylight he crawled out again, drunk as a fiddler."

FIDDLE itself has been in use since the thirteenth century as an informal term for the stuffier-sounding "violin." More than a century ago, FIDDLER'S MONEY referred to any small amount of money, while FIDDLER was the slang equivalent of "cheater or swindler." (Earlier in this century, clothing known as FIDDLE AND FLUTE was, in rhyming slang, a "suit.") The wandering or unsettled FIDDLE-FOOTED of World War II led in the past decade to the clumsy FIDDLE-FISTED.

Perhaps the favorite fiddle phrase, though, was popularized in the 1939 film of *Gone With the Wind,* based on Margaret Mitchell's 1936 novel of the Civil War and Reconstruction. This fiddle term was used repeatedly in the exasperated comments of the story's heroine. In the opening scene, for example, Scarlett O'Hara downplays talk of the coming Civil War with a musical southern dismissal: "FIDDLE-DEE-DEE."

THE BUZZ

In America, the most popular term for social functions, with the potential exception of "party" itself, has long been BEE, perhaps based on the English dialect term "been" for "assistance by neighbors." In turn, that English term may come from the Old English *ben* for "prayer," related to the modern noun "boon."

Bee List

SPINNING BEE a party of women to do spinning of wool for a worthy cause; a Maine newspaper report in 1788 mentioned a noteworthy assembly by "more than one hundred of the fair sex"

APPLE BEE a social event to prepare and dry apples, used in a Harvard rhyme of 1827: "Once Ebenezer Hodge invited me / To help his Dolly at an apple bee"

QUILTING BEE a variant of the 1831 "quilt sitting," cited in 1832: "The females also have similar meetings called 'quilting bees,' when many assemble to work for one, in padding or quilting bed coverings or comforters"

RAISING BEE an obsolete 1833 term (from the earlier "raising") for a house raising and party, with its merits explained in 1852: "the salutary effect of bringing the people together, for the cultivation of friendly feelings, and as large numbers turn out, the work is light to each"

HANGING BEE a facetious 1836 term for a lynching, used in a 1943 history in which "unfortunates paid the full penalty for their crime at a great hanging-bee, held at Mankato, Minnesota, the day after Christmas, 1862"

KISSING BEE an 1853 term for a friendly party of young people; at the turn of the century, a shy traveler described how he "sat in a corner like a homely girl at a kissing-bee"

WOOD BEE a gathering of neighbors to chop wood; used in an 1857 report in which "The whole neighbourhood would assemble to prepare for each other the wood necessary to keep such a fire going during the winter"

SHINGLE BEE the obsolete term for a party to make wooden shingles; a writer in 1868 said that "a 'shingle bee' was held, at night, to expedite work and convince the skeptical that shingles, or anything else, could be made or done, when it had to be"

SPELLING BEE now raised to a national competition each year, an 1872 term for competitive spelling by students; in

1875, a London newspaper identified these wide-spread contests as "a New England invention"

THEATER BEE an obsolete term for a "theater party" (or any group assembled to attend the theater together), first used in an 1897 publication about Harvard

The many types of bees that have aided American work and play, frequently taking on various names, serve to illustrate a change in the national spirit of sociability. While bees were originally meant to provide company in shared work, the modern use of the term refers to a specific type of competition. For example, the National Geographic Bee puts students into a competition for the title of being most knowledgeable about places and place names.

Far more familiar is the SPELLING BEE. In 1998, a twelve-year-old from Jamaica won the latest Scripps Howard National Spelling Bee held in Washington, D.C. The first winner ever from outside the United States, Jody-Anne Maxwell correctly spelled the obscure noun "chiaroscurist," meaning an artist who emphasizes lights and darks, to become the champion of this challenge. This form of competition has also been called a SPELLING FIGHT, as well as a SPELLING MATCH and a SPELLING TOURNAMENT.

Multiple names for any bee are not unusual. Consider the making of maple sugar, known mainly as a SUGAR BEE. Such a gathering has also been called a SUGAR EAT and a SUGAR FIRE, as well as a SUGAR FROLIC, SUGAR LICK, SUGAR PARTY, and SUGAR SUPPER. The celebration in Laura Ingalls Wilder's *Little House in the Big Woods* is known as the SUGARING-OFF DANCE.

The sweetness of those terms, however, may be contrasted with a modern movement toward seeking the privacy that

George Bernard Shaw valued so highly. A generation ago, the writers Helen and Scott Nearing advocated "The Good Life" on their remote farm in New England. At the entrance to their home was posted a no-nonsense schedule: "Our mornings are our own. We'll see visitors 3–5. Help us live the good life—Helen and Scott."

Even less sociable is a current notice above a roaring Georgia river. Local residents, discouraging unexpected visitors, have posted ominous warnings against trespassing. PRIVATE PROPERTY, the sign warns. SURVIVORS WILL BE PROSECUTED.

INTELLECTUALLY SPEAKING

The American Mind

CHAPTER 6

CONFORMITY

$\mathcal{N}$ot all of the characteristics that shape American language are worthy of being celebrated. The trait of conformity, for example, has led the language into frequent and far-reaching repetition of the same idea in the same words. In contrast to independence, conformity is the breeding ground of cliché.

While independence and self-reliance were the traits being uplifted by the essayist Ralph Waldo Emerson in 1841, he noted later in the same decade that Americans had fallen short of those goals. "We are a puny and a fickle folk," Emerson commented in 1849. "Avarice, hesitation, and following are our diseases."

The national need to follow, however, did not end in the nineteenth century. During World War I, the British newspaper magnate Lord Northcliffe attacked what he perceived as the omnipresent need for conformity in American society. "It is impossible for a stranger traveling through the United States," Northcliffe was quoted in 1918, "to tell from the appearance of the people or the country whether he is in Toledo, Ohio, or Portland, Oregon. Ninety million Americans cut their hair in the same way, eat each morning exactly the same breakfast, tie up the small girls' curls with precisely the same kind of ribbon fashioned into bows exactly alike; and in every way all try to look and act as much like all the others as they can."

Such similar thinking allows a straightforward expression to be introduced in one century and extended into a national metaphor by the next. During the Civil War, for instance, the boundary around a prison camp was drawn, and prisoners who crossed that line would be shot for trying to escape. This boundary, known as the "dead line," led to this century's widespread worrying about DEADLINE, now used for a time limit.

WESTWARD, HO!

A film executive, turning down the actor Ronald Reagan for the lead in a 1964 film, expressed the narrow conformity of casting in Hollywood: "Reagan doesn't have the presidential look."

Conventional wisdom has also long held that the newspaper editor Horace Greeley invented the immortal advice of nineteenth-century America: "Go west, young man, go west." Greeley, however, was not the coiner of that phrase. Instead, he did say, "Go west, young man, and grow up with the country," recycling the advice of another editor, John Babson Lane Soule, who had penned the famous words for an 1851 editorial in an Indiana newspaper.

Soule had, in turn, recycled a common expression of the frontier, recorded in an Illinois newspaper in 1834 as "Going West." Although Greeley added the phrase about growing up with the country, he was erroneously assumed by many to have formulated the original expression. In an effort to clear up the misunderstanding, he printed Soule's editorial in his own newspaper, the *New York Tribune,* but many people still insist upon attributing the idea to Horace Greeley. (He was also attributed with the jocular correction that "I never said all Democrats were saloon keepers; what I said was that all saloon keepers were Democrats.")

CONVENTIONAL WISDOM, itself a cliché, does not always ensure accuracy. Coined in 1958 by the economist John Kenneth Galbraith, the phrase began with a pejorative sense that Galbraith attributed to its widespread acceptance by uncritical minds: "It has the approval of those to whom it is addressed."

Popularized by *Newsweek* magazine's "Conventional Wisdom Watch," the term has a generalized connotation of ideas that may have wide acceptance but are sometimes incorrect. CONVENTIONALISTS, however, are not the holders of that wisdom; that noun has been applied since the early nineteenth century to supporters of constitutional conventions, meetings that were intended to adopt or modify state constitutions.

INSIDE CLICHÉ STADIUM

The American language, shaped by the conformity of its users, has adopted many set phrases that, true or not, have been repeated, some for more than a century.

BABY ACT, for instance, was born after the Civil War and applied to anybody who seems childish or immature. The term was still in use after World War II; in 1947, the *Chicago Tribune* editorialized, "In 1935, when the atrocious Wagner law went into effect, did employers and stockholders play the baby act and go on strike?" Improving on immature behavior or making better was TO TAKE THE CUSS OFF, with "cuss" a variant of "curse." In 1843, a New York theatergoer noticed the improved manners and language of the audience when women were in attendance: "The men begun to stream into the theatre like all possessed, with a small sprinkling of the feminine gender, jest enough to take the cuss off and no more."

Getting into trouble was known after the turn of the century as GOING UP A TREE. A 1902 book on slang explains "go up a tree" as "to be in difficulties, like an opossum going up a tree when hunted." An earlier sense of that phrase, however, was much deadlier.

"Go up a tree" in the nineteenth century meant "to be hanged," although the phrase was sometimes shortened to GO UP, a Briticism also referring to a hanging. In 1867, a British book on America related that "Gone up, in the slang of Denver, means gone up a tree. . . . In plain English, the man is said to have been hung." An 1825 book used the shorter form in the story of a captured spy "whose narrow escape, when his brother spy 'went up,' he said, was quite a 'muricle.' " In this century, GOING UP has been used in theatrical slang to denote "forgetting one's lines," a dilemma onstage that the late Irish actress Siobhan McKenna once expressed as "being dry."

GOING TO EXTREMES

Conformity breeds cliché. Several nineteenth-century American expressions about having or losing control have become standards of speech in the twentieth century.

Since the 1830s, TO TAKE A TREE has meant "to hide behind or up in a tree." A more active escape was TO SHOW LEG, meaning "to run off"; it appeared in an 1837 offer of help: "I'll fight for you, or run for you . . . shake fist or show leg." Ten years earlier, a hasty departure was referred to as MAKING TRACKS, a phrase with more staying power. An 1827 book depicted a deserter who "made up his mind to bow his neck and make tracks."

Among phrases for going to extremes is the alliterative BLUE BLAZES. Mason Locke Weems, the early biographer of

George Washington, used this term for excess in an 1818 attack on alcohol: "Ye steep down gulphs of liquid fire! Ye blue blazes of damnation!" Often taken as a term for heat, it nevertheless appeared in a 1934 weather comment that "It was as cold as blue blazes."

Losing control or dying was To Be Off the Handle, now more familiar as To Fly Off the Handle. That phrase is a variant of the 1820 form, To Fly Off the Helve, first recorded in a critique of the orator Henry Clay, who "is almost head-long in his eloquence. To use a back-woods simile, he seems as tho' he would 'fly off the helve,' during the paroxisms of declamation." "Helve" is a centuries-old synonym for "handle," but it is rarely heard in that saying anymore.

A leader's last words often prove to be especially powerful expressions, as in the imperative sentence Don't Give Up the Ship. As he lay dying in 1813, Captain James Lawrence, mortally wounded by the British, exhorted his men aboard the U.S. frigate *Chesapeake* with final words reported as "Don't give up the ship." A longer version of his speech was recorded as "Tell the men to fire faster and not to give up the ship; fight her till she sinks." The British succeeded in capturing the ship, but the words lived on. Thomas Jefferson picked up the idea in an 1816 letter: "My exhortation would rather be 'not to give up the ship.' " Outside of quotation marks, the same idea was expressed by Mark Twain, who wrote in 1892, "We'll not give up the ship yet," and the expression has still not sunk from the language.

Other clichés understate their meanings. The deadly phenomenon called an "earthquake" in Standard English since the fourteenth century was reduced to the slang Shakes during the nineteenth century. "Shakes" was first applied to any countryside marked with the fissures caused by earthquakes and later came to stand for the quake itself. In 1833, Davy Crockett remembered being asked "if I didn't want to go down to the Shakes, and take a bear hunt," and an 1887 newspaper headlined "The Arizona Shake." Better known is the cliché NO GREAT SHAKES for something lacking importance or power. The source of that phrase was shown in its 1837 use in the *New York Mirror:* "Come, Bill, 'taint no use sitting all day on this log—let's take to our axes again—the earthquake's no great shakes after all." Heard less often is the positive form of that cliché, but a Texas magazine commented in 1929 that "Jesse James might be a great guy up in Missouri, but Rube Burrow was 'some shakes' down in Texas."

Once a term becomes widely used, variations on its theme may be many. For instance, money terms frequently used in America include the ALMIGHTY DOLLAR. Washington Irving introduced the term in *The New-Yorker* in 1836: "In a word, the almighty dollar, that great object of universal devotion throughout our land, seems to have no genuine devotees in these peculiar villages." Still in use, the phrase has been stretched in various directions. A California newspaper reported in 1855 that "To-day is 'steamer day,' every body is astir—the immortal dollar is jingling." Other variants include "the immortal half-dollar" in 1866, as well as "the almighty nickel" in 1884 and "the almighty greenback" in 1947.

FOOD FOR THOUGHT

A particularly rich source of American expressions and clichés is the seemingly endless supply of food-related terms. Words and phrases about eating have long been part of the country's vocabulary, reflecting a national obsession with food. These terms also demonstrate the conformity of values and notions in the agrarian society that long held sway throughout the United States.

Patient speakers of the language may recognize the nineteenth-century phrase HOLD YOUR POTATO, an admonishment to "be patient." An 1892 entry in *The Congressional*

Record states, "Now let me beg of the gentleman to hold his potato," a far easier variant of HOLD YOUR HORSES from half a century earlier. For anything hard to believe, the incredulous response of the 1850s was TELL IT TO THE POTATOES. Sometimes called a TATER, the American potato lent itself to other obsolete phrases. Eating a meal back in the 1820s was known as TO SET UP AND SKIN A TATER, and for another version of "that's the truth," there was the 1835 use of THAT'S THE TATER.

Anger has been expressed with various vegetables. A strong attack is GIVING BEANS; in an 1842 commentary, an American soldier reported being "at the battle of New Orleans, when we gave the British beans." MEAN AS BEANS was in use by the Civil War, as in the 1860 admission that "I felt meaner than beans about it." Extreme anger was also portrayed in the nineteenth century with HOT AS AN OLD RADISH.

As another food given a larger meaning, the slang BALONEY for "nonsense" probably came from the large smoked sausage named for the city credited with its origin: Bologna, Italy. That sausage, mentioned in English more than four centuries ago, led to the 1920 use of "baloney" for an untalented prizefighter. *Collier's Magazine* reported in 1920 that "Kane Halliday, alias Kid Roberts, had won his first professional fight by knocking out a boloney with the nom du ring of Young Du Fresne." The "boloney" spelling was popular during the 1920s, but a decade later the spelling "baloney" superseded it.

For a plain or ordinary meal, the frontier term was COMMON DOINGS. A western visitor in 1838 was asked, "Well, stranger, what'll ye take: wheat-bread and chicken fixens, or corn-bread and common doin's?" Southerners have used DINING DAY for fancier foods; in an 1805 letter, the correspondent stated, "If I had time I would give some history of a dining day, of the table and its furniture." Special meals to raise money have been known as the BOX SOCIAL, as well as the BOX PARTY and the BOX SUPPER; a 1929 festival in Elkins, West Virginia, advertised "Old time Fiddling, Banjo, Songs, Pie and Box Social." In 1942, a dialect guide in Maryland defined "box supper" as "an event for raising church or other funds by auctioning box lunches donated by the women of the community."

Dining out has been another source for food terms. Back in 1858, a restaurant was known as an EATING SALOON. That now-obsolete term was not as grandiose, however, as Owen Wister's designation of the restaurant in his 1902 novel, *The Virginian:* "I came upon him one morning in Colonel Cyrus Jones's EATING PALACE." At the other end of the restaurant spectrum is the fast-food outlet, and much earlier than the 1951 FAST-FOOD was the 1903 QUICK LUNCH, an Americanism that soon crossed the Atlantic. *The Chicago Tribune* was amused in 1920 by this transatlantic development: "The first sign of 'crumbling' on the part of the British empire that we have observed is the welcome extended to the 'quick lunch.' "

PET TERMS

In addition to popular terms from food, animals have long supplied the American tongue with wide-ranging expressions. Even Lord Northcliffe resorted to a much older animal metaphor for the conformity of Americans: "They dress alike," he continued his carping, "they talk alike, they think alike. What sheep!"

Animal Clichés

SEE THE ELEPHANT a verb phrase from the early nineteenth century for "to gain worldly experience" or "to become bored with life"

UP TO BEAVER Washington Irving's 1837 phrase to indicate the ability or cunning to outwit a beaver

GONE GOSLING an 1830s variation of the 1830 term "gone goose," for a person who is hopelessly lost or beyond help

WAKE SNAKES an 1848 term for "to get into trouble," used a generation later for "to run away quickly"

CAT-HOOK used in Louisiana since 1850 to identify a fish-hook for catching catfish

WOLF CASTLE an 1850s expression for any area closed in by extremely dense shrubbery

BLUEBIRD a Civil War term for a Union soldier, based on the color of the Northern uniform

BULL OUTFIT not cattle clothing but a nineteenth-century westernism meaning "wagon train," named for the oxen that pulled the wagons

NOT SAY PEATURKEY TO ANYBODY a century-old admonition to keep quiet or not tell a secret

TOAD-STRANGLER a modern colloquialism for any big rain-storm or heavy downpour

The animal term DOG TOWN, for instance, began in 1841 as a capitalized name: "This is emphatically a Dog Town, a town literally overrun by dogs." Soon it was used as a Westernism for any colony or community of prairie dogs. An 1843 visitor to the West commented, "We are now past all the dog towns . . . saw plenty on the South Platte." A century later the National Park Service reported in 1942 that "the huge 'dog towns' of fifty years ago are present only in the memories of grizzled old-timers." Theater slang picked up the term and tried it out in 1898 with a special application: "Washington is becoming quite a 'dog town,' as theatrical people call a city in which they 'try on' plays before bringing them to New York."

Less favorable is the Americanism CROOKED AS A DOG'S HIND LEG. The language journal *Dialect Notes* traces that colloquial phrase meaning "very crooked or unfair" to a 1903 use in Missouri. In 1920, Sinclair Lewis employed the term in his novel *Main Street* to describe a dishonest character: "Terry is crooked as a dog's hind leg." A Southernism that began as a put-down of a small dog is the noun FEIST, leading to the adjective FEISTY for acting quarrelsome or showing spunk. George Washington used a variant spelling of the adjective to represent in his 1770 diary "a small foist looking yellow cur." As a possible source of "feist" or FICE DOG, the British "fisting hound" was based on an obsolete verb for "to break wind." *The Congressional Globe* in 1842 reported that "Private individuals were bull-dogged—or fice-dogged, if the gentleman pleases." The more familiar "feisty," now sometimes used to denote an admirable quality, was defined as a Southernism in a folksy 1913 lexicon: "Feisty means when a feller's allers wigglin' about, wantin' ever'body to see him, like a kid when the preacher comes." During the past two centuries, the term has transferred from pets to people who show the characteristics of the fice dog.

Other animal phrases have also been used to express unappealing traits. The burrowing GOPHER, its name perhaps from the French *gaufre* for "honeycomb" to suggest its digging patterns, has been employed to indicate deceit. A naturalist visiting the West in 1870, for example, introduced GOPHER-ING FELLOW into print: "In California, a man who practices deception, or acts in an underhanded manner, is sometimes called a 'gophering fellow.' " BE THE GOAT has also been around for more than a century, with the specific sense of "to take the blame"; this phrase uses a shortening of "scapegoat," with a victimized New Yorker explaining in 1894 that "I was in for no less a scheme than actually smuggling a cargo . . . for no other reason than 'to be the goat.' "

Not all animal expressions, however, are negative. THE GOOSE HANGS HIGH came into the lexicon during the Civil War with an upbeat sense that prospects are encouraging or bright. An 1863 song's chorus announced, "Oh! you bet your bogus dollars, / Oh! you bet, the goose hangs high." By a generation later, the same phrase was used to contrast illusion with economic reality in *The Congressional Record* during 1894: "If you believe there is a plethora of money, if you believe everything is lovely and the goose hangs high, go down to the soup houses in the city of New York." Some historians believe the phrase comes from the placement of the goose in a butcher shop, but another theory holds that it is a variant of "the goose honks high," suggesting that in good weather the goose flies at a higher altitude.

Horses have received varying treatment in the language. "Where sense is wanting," Benjamin Franklin noted in *Poor Richard's Almanack* in 1754, "everything is wanting," and since the 1830s, that notion of "good old-fashioned common sense" has been known by the favorable label of HORSE SENSE. It first appeared in print in an 1832 book about workers along the Ohio River: "He's a man of good strong horse sense"; by 1850, the term was widely recognized as a Westernism. Even more intimate is HITCHING HORSES, a term for marriage equivalent to GETTING HITCHED (Mark Twain used HITCHING TEAMS TOGETHER for "joining forces"). The *Massachusetts Spy* in 1830 reported an unromantic exchange that began, "Your notions and mine don't agree; we can never hitch horses." To that statement came a quick rejoinder: "Who asked you to hitch horses?"

The same animal, however, took on an unflattering slang term in 1904 for its eating habits: HAY-BURNER. A Chicago newspaper calculated in 1945 that "On the basis of the old

World War I formula . . . one hay burner was equivalent to five soldiers." Animal and food terms have combined in other ways, as in LONG FOOD; an 1823 order for farm supplies included "as much corn or oats and hay and fodder as our horses can destroy (usually half a bushel of grain and a rackful of long food)." The farming term for "heavy" is GRASS-BELLIED, while GRASS WATER refers to swampy areas or to the Everglades.

Chickens have also been the objects of varied additions to the language. During the past century, Westerners referred to a feather-stuffed comforter as a HENSKIN. In 1902, a disgruntled visitor to the West asked irritatedly, "Why don't you burn these henskins and get you a decent bed?" Since the Civil War, anything extremely hard to find has been described as being SCARCE AS HEN'S TEETH. *American Speech* has tracked MAD AS A WET HEN to an 1823 usage, and a chicken product has taken the fanciful name of HEN FRUIT for more than a century. *Harper's Magazine* described an incident that occurred in a Maine restaurant in 1854: "A young lady is said to have asked a gentleman at the table of a hotel 'down East' to pass her the 'hen fruit.' She pointed to a plate of eggs."

The hibernating practices of other animals added the phrase DEN UP. Used primarily about bears, it means "to hibernate," as in retreating to an animal's den for the winter. In 1843, a pioneer describing Canada explained the phrase: "In that climate the bears usually den up in the winter, and lie in something of a torpid state." Before the end of the nineteenth century, the phrase had also been transferred to lethargic people. "Our people . . . are inclined to 'den up' in the hot weather," a northern writer suggested in 1894, "as certain animals . . . do in the cold season." Other users of the term point to the similar practice of snakes.

Far less savory is the phrase SHEEP NANNY TEA. In the hills of Kentucky, that term was applied to a favorite folk recipe, defined as "a tea made from sheep droppings." In

1873, a local history remarked about this Kentucky cure that "Then sheep-nannie tea was prescribed; about a quart of that condiment swallowed down at night was certain to effect a cure." Not limited to Kentucky, however, the concoction Down East took the name of NANNY-PLUM TEA. A 1937 work on folk medicine pointed out the intention of this hot drink: "One remedy there is, peculiar to the heart of Maine, I hope. That is the laxative nanny-plum tea. You find nanny plums where the sheep have marched on their narrow track through the ferns." The writer of that report adds, "It is, they say, efficacious."

As Ralph Waldo Emerson warned his readers in 1856, "You must pay for conformity," adding that "All goes well as long as you run with conformists." Conformity of language leads too easily into cliché and the recycling of old expressions, but not all recycling is to be avoided. The ultimate recycling may be an epitaph that Benjamin Franklin once composed for himself. After his death in 1790, Franklin's actual epitaph was a short Latin phrase that lacked the inventiveness of this earlier version:

> The body of
> Benjamin Franklin, printer,
> (Like the covers of an old book,
>   Its contents worn out,
> And strippt of its leathering and gilding)
>   Lies here, food for worms!
> Yet the work itself shall not be lost,
> For it will, as he believed, appear once more,
>   In a new
> And more beautiful edition,
>   Corrected and amended
>   By its author!

CHAPTER 7

CREATIVITY

"*J*eet?"
"No, joo?"

This shorthand discussion of lunch plans—"jeet?" means "did you eat?" and "joo?" is an elided form of "did you?"—recurs daily in neighborhoods across America. Several years ago, it was described as "the quintessential Chicago conversation" by Mike Royko, the popular *Chicago Tribune* columnist who died in 1997. In recent years, however, this lunchtime elision (actually an example of "pronunciation spelling"—the spelling of terms according to how they are spoken—and technically not slang) has spread about the nation, with widespread claims to locating its origin across the United States.

Slang itself is often equally uncertain in origin, but it marks the most creative act in language formation. The American writer Carl Sandburg provided a particularly vivid description of this characteristic of our national tongue. "Slang," wrote the poet, who died in 1967, "is a language that rolls up its sleeves, spits on its hands, and goes to work."

As a language historian, H. L. Mencken shared Sandburg's

passion for the slang terms of the United States. In his work *The American Language,* Mencken commented that "Americans seem to be vastly more adept at making new slang than Englishmen." He added, "There was a time when this was not true, and most of the slang that American purists frowned upon was of English origin, but after the War of 1812 and the beginning of the great movement into the West, Americans began to roll their own."

SLINGING SLANG

Slang, one of the most difficult language terms to define, has long been creating much of the American vocabulary.

The etymology of the 1756 noun SLANG is unknown. Clearly unrelated, though, is another American use of "slang," now considered obsolete but recorded in *Notes & Queries* in 1890 by a traveler who explained: "I remember in the Adirondacks, a boatable channel or stream connecting a small lake with the Raquette river. Our boatman called it 'the Slang.' He could not tell me whether slang was a proper name, or a common noun." The source of that use is easily traced to the Dutch *slang,* which means "water hose or pipe."

J. E. Lighter is in the process of collecting the country's contributions into the multivolume *Random House Historical Dictionary of American Slang.* In this monumental reference work, the brief definition offered for "slang" is "an informal, nonstandard, nontechnical vocabulary composed chiefly of novel-sounding synonyms for standard words and phrases." Lighter helpfully adds that "the use of slang suggests, as standard speech cannot, an intimate familiarity with a referential object or idea (compare, for example, the difference between *professional dancer* and *hoofer, wait tables* and *sling hash, prison* and *the joint, beer* and *suds, intellectual* and *wonk*)."

Americans have been fascinated by slang since the early

days of the colonies. Out of New England came SLANGWHANG, a rhyming term for political talk that proves to be nonsense. In this compound, WHANG may be a synonym for the noun "twang" or for the verb "to toss." In 1807, Washington Irving's satirical publication *Salmagundi* introduced the term SLANG-WHANGER to depict editors as knights. "These knights, denominated editors, or slang-whangers," Irving wrote, ". . . may be said to keep up a constant firing 'in words.' " A journalism critic commented in 1839 that "Two of the Nashville papers . . . are getting to be uncommonly interesting, at least to those of their patrons who like to see papers filled with nothing but political slang-whangery."

As recently as 1950, *The Chicago Tribune* still applied the term to the work of advertising copywriters: "The titles 'Ice Capades' and 'Borscht Capades' are examples of the numerous blends and portmanteau words spawned by slang-whangers and by Advertisea, the tenth Muse." Current concern about the attack terms of mudslinging political campaigns may second a Buffalo newspaper's 1904 call for "a clean campaign—one free from gross personal abuse and slang-whanging."

DUCKS TO SNOWBIRDS

A survey of the creative slang and slangwhanging used in America reveals a wealth of words added to our national tongue, although much of the origins of American slang remains obscure.

The general substitution of DUCK for "person" or "guy," for instance, may be traced back to 1846, but the reason for that slang use remains unclear, even though the phrase "odd duck" is still heard. Since the turn of the century, DUCK FIT has indicated a fit of temper. The humorist Joel Chandler Harris recorded the term in 1900: "I said as much to Horace Greeley, and he and his friends had a good many duck-fits about it." The term was still hyphenated a few years later in a short story by O. Henry.

More understandable is the slang use of GRIT UP, a verb phrase meaning "to gather grit or nerve." *Harper's Magazine* in 1890 offered the view of a new employee that "I see I must jest grit up for I'd got a big job o' work." Half a century earlier, the adjective GRITTY meant "full of grit," particularly as a sign of anger. Since the start of the nineteenth century, GRIT itself was slang for physical courage, popularized again in this century by the title of the John Wayne western based on the 1968 Charles Portis novel, *True Grit*.

Also familiar to modern audiences is the slang use of IN-DEEDY as an emphatic form of the shorter "indeed." Back in 1856, *Knickerbocker Magazine* printed the comment of "Yes, indeedy," and the phrase is still widely heard.

Often the meaning of a slang phrase depends upon the word that follows the verb. FREEZE DOWN, for example, has been a slang phrase for "to settle or establish" since 1840. When the particle in that phrase changed from "down" to "in," the slang sense changed; since 1876, FREEZE IN has meant "to join or become part," and FREEZE OUT has been used for "to exclude" since 1861. During the 1840s, FREEZE all by itself gained a now-obsolete slang sense of "to yearn for or desire." The similar YEN did not enter the language until 1906; derived from a Chinese phrase for "opium craving," "yen" as noun and verb has stuck as a slang term while "freeze" has disappeared.

Slang may develop centuries later than the standard sense of a term. SNOWBIRD dates back to 1674 for a junco or other bird seen primarily during the wintertime. In the twentieth century, however, the term has taken on various slang senses. The *New York Evening Post* reported in 1905 on military desertions: "28 per cent. deserted after three months, and were presumably 'snowbirds,' that is, men who enlist to get food and clothing during the winter months." Since 1914 the term has referred to a habitual user of cocaine, and since 1923, "snowbird" has also applied to any Northerner who travels south for good weather during the winters.

STAGE AND SCHOOL

Over the past century, America's slangsters have created both negative and positive terms for theatrical folk and bookish students.

The leading negative noun is STOOGE, which may be related to "stage" although its origin is not known with certainty. The poet Robert Service used the term in 1945 to explain an experience he had onstage before the turn of the century. A stage musician hired Service to take the stage first and play miserably; then the musician played, his performance enhanced by Service's failure.

That sense of "stooge" as "stage assistant" was first recorded in print by the *Saturday Evening Post* in 1913: "Ben, I want you to plant one of your stooges in that coop with a couple of smoke-pots, so that we'll get the effect of Jack coming through the thickest of it." The image of ineptness onstage led a generation later to the physical humor of the Three Stooges.

A more complimentary example of stage slang, ANGEL, tracks its use to underworld slang. Since 1882, "angel" has been used for somebody naive or innocent enough to become the victim of swindling. From that idea of victimization developed a much kinder sense of a person generous enough to provide financing for a stage production.

In a police report of 1897 appeared the sense of victim: "The leading lady of the company had a bald-headed angel on the string." That sense continued in a 1902 study of language, in which "angel" is defined as "a man who innocently backs unprofitable or questionable enterprises to the profit of the promoters solely. It is a term of contempt." By 1909, the term had gained its more positive connotation, when another dictionary explained the term as "a nonprofessional financier backer of a play or other amusement enterprise."

School slang, which has in recent years used TOOL and WONK as terms for the overly studious, added the negative term SPOOPS to the American language more than a century ago. In 1851, a collector of college words noted, "At Harvard College, a weak, silly fellow, or one who is disliked on account of his foolish actions, is called a spoops." That noun of unknown origin apparently made the rounds of the colleges, because it appeared almost a decade later in the *Yale Literary Magazine*. At Yale, the term was applied in 1860 to a boring student; whenever such a student "makes a dull recitation, he is denominated a regular 'spoops.' "

In this century, "L7" has been used by students and rock musicians as a term for somebody who is overly conventional. Written in block letters, the "L" and the "7" suggest the shape of a SQUARE, popularized in the 1960s as a derogation of anybody considered too rigid or conservative.

Terms that sound alike may exchange meanings in slang. The homophones WHIZ and WIZ come from different sources, but they are used interchangeably at times. Since the turn of the century, "wiz" has been a clipped form of "wizard," based on the Middle English *wys,* meaning "wise." The longer "whiz," on the other hand, is probably imitative of the sound of fast movement. *Harper's Magazine* introduced the slang "whiz" for "political celebration" in an 1892 commentary on "The prevailing American desire to indulge in what is widely known as an electoral whiz, accompanied by high stepping and a feeling of great wealth."

By World War II, WHIZ KID referred positively to any sharp student, celebrated today for a specialty such as "math whiz" or "computer whiz."

STRAIGHT TALK

The creativity of slang in America has often produced more than one term for the same meaning. THE STRAIGHT has been used for factual information since the Civil War, but by the 1890s, STRAIGHT GOODS was another expression for "the truth."

CHIN also dates back to the Civil War as a slang term, specifically meaning "talk"; since 1877, the reduplication CHIN-CHIN has also meant "talk" and perhaps came from Chinese pidgin. Small talk has been called CHIN-JAW since World War II, much more recent than the 1883 adjective CHINNY for "talkative." Small-town talk or gossip has led to other slang terms for nosy neighbors. Almost two centuries ago, a slang phrase for gossip was STREET YARN, and in 1859, Bartlett identified as "a woman's word" the phrase STARE CAT, which he defined as "a woman or girl who amuses herself with gazing at her neighbors."

Occasionally, however, a slang term contradicts an earlier sense with a new meaning, much as the negative BAD became an admiring adjective in Black English a century ago. Similarly, WIDE-OPEN as a neutral adjective for "unlimited or without restriction" dates back to 1852. By the end of the nineteenth century, though, the same term was being used to describe overt criminal activity. In 1896, Theodore Roosevelt commented, "By February everything would again 'be running wide open.' . . . The gambler, the disorderly-house keeper, and the law breaking liquor-seller would be plying their trades once more." More than half a century later, a Nebraska publication editorialized that "In the field of municipal government, a myth has been developed and sustained in many cities that a wide-open town policy is good business."

The negative sense of that slang term, however, was overturned in a 1960s phrase supporting freedom of speech and debate: UNINHIBITED, ROBUST AND WIDE-OPEN. In a 1964

Supreme Court decision, Associate Justice William J. Brennan Jr. introduced that phrase in deciding a libel case. "We consider this case," Brennan said, "against the background of a profound national commitment to the principle that debate on public issues should be uninhibited, robust and wide-open."

GLUG, GLUG, GLUG

In the history of American slang, drinking and alcohol have been perhaps the most creative sources for new terms.

Drinking Up

RAILROAD a kind of liquor mentioned in Philadelphia in 1835: "The pair were well acquainted with that species of liquor now styled 'Railroad,' and vended at three cents a glass"

FOOL'S WATER an 1837 term explained by a Missouri writer: "The disturber, . . . by the Indians appropriately named 'fire-water,' and more emphatically 'fool-water' "

HARDWARE used in 1839 as a synonym for "hard liquor," probably intended to mislead the hearer: "He prepared to swallow his fifth invoice of 'hardware' "

VETO an obsolete 1841 term from New Orleans for a hard drink: "Taylor is an honest Democrat—he ordered a veto, the latest invented and most approved beverage"

MIXOLOGIST an 1856 substitute for the 1836 "bartender":

"Who ever heard of a man's . . . calling the barkeeper a mixologist of tipicular fixins?"

BUSTHEAD inferior whisky that was mentioned in a San Francisco newspaper in 1857: "A big strapping six-footer, full of 'bust head,' . . . slapped his fists together, swearing he was 'spiling for a fight' "

BAYOU BLUE the reverse of "Blue Bayou," a 1977 Linda Ronstadt song title, this term for an alcoholic drink provoked an 1870 fantasy: "He thought (especially if he had taken a little 'bayou blue') he would weigh several ton"

RAZZLE-DAZZLE the title of a song in the 1977 Broadway musical *Chicago,* this rhyming compound was used in 1889 to describe a state of intoxication: "A Kansas paper . . . recently told of a 'regular old razooper, who, having got a skate on, indulged in a glorious razzle-dazzle' "

WARNING an appropriately named drink, the term was used in Maryland in 1908: "The Major looked out at the suburbs of Baltimore over his before-luncheon 'warning' "

VOTING JUICE a 1919 phrase, perhaps inspired by the preceding "veto," for liquor used in the influence of voting: "By the time the first barrel of 'voting juice' was empty, all had voted"

Long before NOSE CANDY became a term for cocaine in the twentieth century, liquor had taken the slang name of NOSE PAINT; a Colorado visitor in 1881 related, "We saw . . . a sign, in which the name which I have never encountered elsewhere was given to stimulating beverages. This sign was 'Nosepaint and Lunch.' " Fifty years earlier the language had picked up the term O-BE-JOYFUL as another name for hard liquor; after its first appearance in 1831, it appeared almost a century later in a 1914 issue of *Dialect Notes,* along with the variant spelling OH-BE-JOYFUL and an alternative name, OH-BE-RICH-AN'-HAPPY.

In the United States, a pronunciation spelling of LIQUOR created the rural variant LICKER. The humorist Irvin Cobb offered a definition of "corn licker" for the Distillers' Code Authority in the early twentieth century. Here are Cobb's revelations on the effects of such moonshine: "It smells like gangrene starting in a mildewed silo, it tastes like the wrath to come, and when you absorb a deep swig of it you have all the sensations of having swallowed a lighted kerosene lamp. A sudden, violent jolt of it has been known to stop the victim's watch, snap his suspenders and crack his glass eye right across." Familiar slang terms for that liquor include REDEYE and ROTGUT to suggest other effects of these beverages on the body.

Not all slang terms about drinking practices are easy to track back to their origins. SPEAKEASY gained popularity as any shop for illicit whiskey during Prohibition, but it is by no means established that this slang term came from American English. In fact, H. L. Mencken included this detailed footnote in his first supplement to *The American Language:* "Eric Partridge suggested in the London *Times Literary Supplement* that the term 'may have been suggested by the English SPEAK-SOFTLY-SHOP, a significant underworld term for a smuggler's house at which liquor could be inexpensively obtained.' Partridge traced this English term to 1823. [Richard] Thornton lists speak-easy, but without attempting to trace it in American usage. He says that it 'seems to belong to Philadelphia'—on what ground, I do not know."

There is more certainty about the earlier forms, BLIND PIG

and BLIND TIGER. These slang terms for a place of illegal liquor sales were explained in an 1857 newspaper: "I sees a kinder pigeon-hole cut in the side of a house, and over the hole, in big writin', 'Blind Tiger, ten cents a sight.' . . . Says I to the feller inside, 'here's your ten cents, walk out your wildcat.' Stranger, instead of showin' me a wild varmint without eyes, I'll be dodd-busted if he didn't shove out a glass of whiskey. You see, that 'blind tiger' was an arrangement to evade the law, which won't let 'em sell licker there, except by the gallon."

These terms add variety and force to American speech, and names of drinks have become part of the nation's history. At the annual Mountain Man Trade Fair in Santa Fe, New Mexicans gather to commemorate the courage of nineteenth-century trappers in overcoming the hardships of winters in the Rocky Mountains. In the spring, these trappers would come down from the mountains in search of company and provisions, and the celebration included a favorite beverage. Known as the HAILSTORM, this powerful drink was an early version of the mint julep.

Other drinks have also taken on metaphorical names. SUDDEN DEATH, a fourteenth-century phrase that is now used in sports for a tiebreaking period, was mentioned by Mark Twain, who wrote in an 1865 sketch that "we had . . . kept out of sight and full of chain-lightning, sudden death and scorpion-bile all day." TANGLEFOOT, an 1859 term for inferior whiskey, led to the slang TANGLELEGGED to depict a state of inebriation. James Fenimore Cooper introduced the now-obsolete phrase WESTERN COMFORT for whiskey in an 1827 novel: "I will engage to get the brats acclimated to a fever-and-ague bottom in a week, and not a word shall be uttered harder to pronounce than the bark of a cherry-tree, with perhaps a drop or two of western comfort." The hyphenated HALF-AND-HALF is now a term for a combination of milk and cream, but in

1835 it was recorded with this recipe: " 'half whisky, half cider-brandy, and no MISTAKE,' a word which in the preparation of this libation represents water."

America's most creative language has long celebrated the potency of its potables. A Santa Barbara, California, newspaper complained in 1857 that "The drinks ain't no good here—there ain't no variety in them, neither; no white-nose, apple-jack, stone-wall, chain-lightning." Benjamin Franklin may have been the first American to collect the many and varied terms for drunkenness, printing over two hundred of them on the front page of his *Pennsylvania Gazette* in 1737.

The most successful collector, however, is Paul Dickson of Garrett Park, Maryland, whose extensive list earned him a Guinness record for collecting the most synonyms for a single term. In fact, he is credited with 2,660 synonyms for "drunk," and the creative collection continues to grow.

CHAPTER 8

ENTERPRISE

"The chief business of the American people is business," Calvin Coolidge has long been quoted as saying.

"Silent Cal" they called him. Soft-spoken Calvin Coolidge, the thirtieth president of the United States, earned the nickname for his exaggerated reticence. The last president regularly to compose his own speeches, he was good for the occasional pithy saying ("If you don't say anything, you won't be called on to repeat it") or terse summary (asked about a preacher's sermon on sin, Coolidge replied, "He said he was against it"). But nowhere else did he demonstrate his understanding of how America works as concisely as in his 1925 speech to the Society of American Newspaper Editors, when he identified business itself as the electorate's chief business.

That business, in fact, extends back to ancient Americans. A recent study shows that farming in America began more than three millennia ago, much earlier than previously believed. The growth of America's business language, however, has been primarily a modern development.

BARGAIN JARGON

A large part of the American vocabulary over the past three centuries has been the addition of business jargon and financial terms. At the center of this development is the name of a short roadway in downtown Manhattan. Coming to represent the American economy, that enterprising stretch of pavement has been known since colonial days as WALL STREET.

Named for a wall that ran alongside the street during the Dutch settlement of the city, Wall Street appeared in print in an 1806 remembrance: "Walking thro' Wall street yesterday morning, I saw a large crowd." Three decades later came the earliest citation to indicate the financial importance of the street. A Jamestown, New York, newspaper reported in 1836 that "A company—Wall street brokers and speculators—are the applicants for the loan to the New York and Erie Railroad." From the street's name was derived a term for the financiers who speculate there: Wall Streeters, found in print since the late nineteenth century.

Foremost among other business terms provided by the Dutch is the noun BOSS, based on the Dutch *baas,* or master. The term was used in American versions of the Dutch word by the middle of the 1600s, as "boss" went through such spelling variations as "base" and "bass." The modern spelling was in effect by the early nineteenth century. Washington Irving reported an embarrassing work incident in an 1806 admission: "I had completely forgotten the errand, . . . so I had to return, make an awkward apology to boss, and look like a nincompoop." The term, used often in the twentieth century as an adjective meaning "superior or excellent," was already common by the 1830s (as in "a boss shoemaker") to indicate someone of higher rank.

Responsibilities of that boss include RIDING HERD, a Westernism in use for the past century. Those who originated "riding herd" were the cowboys who guarded cattle by staying on the edge of a herd. Figuratively, the term came to mean any close watch or observation with frequent interruption or correction. When an employee proved unsuitable, the American vocabulary added the slang GIVE THE AIR as a synonym for "to fire without paying." That verb phrase came out of show business; in 1928, an entertainer who displeased the boss was reported to have "got himself in bad with the great man . . . and was given the air before the engagement was over." Even earlier was the still frequent CANNED, predating World War I; the unkind source of this term for "dismissed" was the image of tying a can to the tail of an animal before chasing it away.

FUNNY BUSINESS

Enterprising coiners have provided a number of business terms, not only for coins themselves but also for those who make a living.

Out of Spanish came an addition to America's business slang, with a coin called BIT OF EIGHT in English. Eight bits formed a dollar, with TWO BITS equivalent to a quarter. Originally two bits—still heard in the musical catchphrase "Shave and a haircut, two bits!"—referred to two separate coins, but the Americanism endured when the quarter became a single coin. A southern visitor's diary entry of 1730 reported that "I saw peach trees in ye blossom and many delightful varieties. Cost me two bitts."

Inflation led from the westernism BIT HOUSE for a saloon (an Illinois paper recorded in 1839 that "It is a bit a drink at the genteel drunkeries") to the designation of "two-bit" for something inexpensive (a San Francisco newspaper reported, "The only 'let up' to their speed was when they stopped to 'smile,' which they did at every 'two bit house' on the road"). The modern use of the modifier "two-bit" arrived by the turn of the century. A 1904 issue of the *New York Evening Post* confided, "Out in the 'two-bits' country, on the other side of the Rocky Mountains, it is still possible to pass Confederate paper money if the swindler goes about it in a cool, nonchalant way." Politicians latched on to the modifier as an attack term. In 1945, a newspaper editorial dismissed "the two-bit politicians of Maryland who can pass or block almost any legislation."

Other business-related language came from the names of coins. The slang phrase NOT WORTH A PLUGGED (or PLUG) NICKEL came from a British use of the verb "plug," which indicates a way to devalue a coin by removing its metal core and replacing it with something inferior. In this century, "plugged nickel" became a common variant of the alliterative PLUGGED PESO. Similarly, the 1935 PENNY-PINCHING as a term for frugality suggested a cheapness that went beyond the earlier (1916) NICKEL NURSER. That expression appeared in a 1924 issue of *Cosmopolitan* with a variant spelling of the five-cent coin: "A proper nickle-nurser, what I mean!"

American business has found many other ways to derogate its participants. The priest or prophet among American Indians was known as a MEDICINE MAN, a term later applied to the lead figure in traveling medicine shows. That peddler of tonics also took the name of ESSENCE PEDDLER, mentioned by the novelist Nathaniel Hawthorne in 1838: "He was not exclusively an essence-peddler, having a large tin box, which had been filled with dry goods, combs, jewelry, &c., now mostly sold out." TRAVELING SALESMAN was added to the language by 1885.

Lawyers have been devalued for almost two centuries as SLEEPING ATTORNEYS and for more than a century as AMBULANCE CHASERS. The earlier phrase appeared by 1809 and was based on paying an attorney to sleep where a jury has been lodged in order to influence their decision in a case; an observer of this unethical practice admitted in the early 1800s that "It has been found that a sleeping attorney may be rendered very profitable." Similarly unscrupulous is the later phrase; an issue of *The Congressional Record* in 1897 reported, "In New York City there is a style of lawyers known to the profession as 'ambulance chasers,' because they are on hand wherever there is a railway wreck, or a street-car collision, or a gasoline explosion."

More appealing is the KISS DEPOSITOR, still part of the assembly line in making the popular chocolate candy in Hershey, Pennsylvania.

MAKING CHANGE

"When the going gets tough," reads a popular bumper sticker, "the tough go shopping!" Shoppers and business owners have also been responsible for a variety of America's business talk.

Candy was only one product to be found in the business known as the GENERAL STORE. That label has been in use since the early nineteenth century for any store with a general assortment of goods for sale, ranging from food and snuff to lanterns and bolts of fabric. An 1835 visitor to Virginia admired "a neat village with considerable trade, and containing 16 dwelling houses, 3 general stores, 2 groceries."

By the middle of the twentieth century came the much larger SUPERMARKET. That term, first used in 1933, led a magazine writer in 1946 to the nostalgic notion that "It was only a step from his giant supermarket to the crossroads store where Grandmother traded eggs for tea." More recent is the MEGASTORE, offering an even larger array of products in a single establishment. Today's disappearing FIVE-AND-TEN-CENT STORE, now giving way to the higher-priced DOLLAR STORE, was preceded by the even less expensive CENT SHOP, a store in Salem, Massachusetts, described by Nathaniel Hawthorne in his 1851 novel, *The House of the Seven Gables*.

With a standard eight-hour day as part of a forty-hour

week, workers in stores no longer have to endure the TEN-HOUR workday. That British-based modifier, though, was the standard being sought when Martin Van Buren explained in a presidential message of 1840 that "The President of the United States . . . directs that all such persons, whether laborers or mechanics, be required to work only the number of hours prescribed by the ten-hour system." Thankfully, the modifier "ten-hour" is now identified in dictionaries of business jargon as "historical."

Putting too much time into any enterprise led to extended historical uses of WIDOW and WIDOWER. In British dialect, a GRASS WIDOW was a rejected mistress or a wife temporarily abandoned, and an AMERICAN WIDOW referred to a woman whose husband had left England for America. In America, the term became CALIFORNIA WIDOW, popularized by the gold rush in the middle of the nineteenth century. John Bartlett explained in 1877 that " 'California widow' . . . came into use during the rush to California, 1850 to 1860, when the newfound treasures of that country separated so many husbands from their wives." The prospector who left his wife to head west became recognized in California as a SPIRITUAL WIDOWER. With the advent of the Civil War came the term WAR WIDOW for any woman whose spouse was still alive but was gone to the battlefield. For the past two decades, a more jocular usage has been in play for any woman married to a fanatic watcher of games being played on television: FOOTBALL WIDOW.

BUGGED

Not all the coinages from American enterprise have been complimentary.

Another historical term, used to indicate the business advantage of great wealth, is the slang MONEY BUG, referring to an extremely rich person. The short story writer O. Henry commented in 1904 that "The chief had got together the same old crowd of money bugs with pink faces and white vests to see us march in." That slang use of BUG followed an earlier slang meaning of "person showing enthusiasm or obsession"; an 1841 congressional report stated that "Mr. Alford of Georgia warned the 'tariff bugs' of the South that . . . he would read them out of church." In the nineteenth century, anybody wealthy or important was known as a BIG BUG, used both in England and in the United States, while the American aristocracy formed a BIG BUGOCRACY. (BUGOLOGY was an 1843 term for those who could not remember "entomology.") BUG-EATER, on the other hand, was an Americanism for somebody unimportant; that southernism of the 1850s was mentioned in an 1878 magazine article about western words: "in Rocky Mountain parlance, a worthless fellow is called a 'bug eater.' "

Other uncomplimentary terms have developed in American business. The slang TIGHTWAD, for example, dates back to the turn of the century and is based on the image of the owner's money being gathered in a wad too tight to be parted with, based on the use during the early nineteenth century of "wad" for a roll of dollar bills. The humorist George Ade helped introduce the term; in 1900, Ade wrote (with his trademark eccentric use of capital letters) of a miserly character that "Henry was undoubtedly the Tightest Wad in the Township."

In the hotel business, tightwads who failed to pay their living expenses led to the phrase RUN ONE'S BOARD. In 1897, the novelist William Dean Howells used the expression to describe those who try to absquatulate: "It will be quite enough for the hotel-keeper if they run their board. I shall have to pay for it." Running out on the debt led to the slang phrase PEEL IT, meaning "to run away at full speed." Another term for a hasty departure was CUT DIRT, heard in an 1820s song.

Still familiar is the 1920s noun GIMMICK, used originally

for a small device that is used secretly. A 1928 issue of *American Speech* mentioned the term among carnival tricks to deceive the public: "Gimmick—The brake, tip-up, or other device used on games of chance to make them crooked or unfair to the towner who plays them." By extension, the term gained a sense of "sneaky scheme" as well as "selling point," popularized by a Jule Styne/Stephen Sondheim song from the 1959 musical *Gypsy,* which provides potential strippers with the musical advice "You Gotta Have a Gimmick."

Even more negative is the name for a dishonest transaction that evoked a familiar noun and verb. When change is returned in a purchase and falls short of the proper amount, the money returned is known as SHORT CHANGE. That noun phrase was used by the American novelist Upton Sinclair in 1908, five years after the first appearance of the verb form, TO SHORTCHANGE, "to return less than the correct amount." Also heard in circus and carnival contexts, the term was applied in Oklahoma after World War II to the lack of enterprise in public arts education; a 1948 editorial complained that "School boards and school administrations are short-changing the children of America by failing to sponsor school orchestras."

YANKEE-PANKEE

Since the eighteenth century, American enterprise has been variously excoriated as "Yankee trickery" and hailed as "Yankee ingenuity," although no one has been ingenious enough to discover the root of the term YANKEE. Theories, however, abound for the formation, long a subject of scholarly study and skepticism.

Yankeeisms

YANKEEFIED a Revolutionary War colloquialism for "made to behave like a Yankee," used a century ago to comment that "Japan is getting Yankeefied in more ways than one"

JOHN YANKEE a personification of the typical American; John Adams championed the name in a 1778 letter, declaring his patriotism: "I never was however much of John Bull. I was John Yankee and such I shall live and die"

ANGLO-YANKEE a pejorative term for New Englanders who were considered to be unduly under England's influence, even halfway through the nineteenth century

CONNECTICUT YANKEE since the 1850s, any Yankee from Connecticut, with a reputation for being cunning, and made famous by the title of the 1889 Mark Twain novel, *A Connecticut Yankee in King Arthur's Court*

HOMEMADE YANKEE a contemptuous Civil War term for any Southerner who remained loyal to the Union

YANKEE GRIT dating back to the Civil War, a term for determination or persistent courage

YANKEEDOM a southern colloquialism from the nineteenth century for New England, also known as "Yankeeland"

PLAY YANKEE WITH a nineteenth-century verb phrase meaning "to cheat or mislead" (in 1896, *The Congressional Record* included this explanation of the phrase: "Now I will play Yankee with my friend. . . . I will answer his question by asking another")

Enterprise

> **NORTH CAROLINA YANKEE** a twentieth-century nickname used locally in South Carolina for any hardworking farmer who has moved there from North Carolina
>
> **YANKEENESS** a noun used by the short-story writer O. Henry after the turn of the century for "the quality or state of being like a Yankee"

Some insist that the natives who witnessed the arrival of the colonists in New England tried to pronounce "English" and came no closer than "Yankee." New Englanders invented a mythical tribe of Massachusetts Indians known as the "Yankos," which meant "Invincibles," whom the colonists conquered and then took their name. Virginia's colonists, in an angry response, pointed to the Cherokee word *eankke,* meaning "coward," as the true source, because the New Englanders failed to assist the Virginians in fighting the Cherokees.

More likely, the term resulted from the Dutch designation of "Jan Kaas," or "John Cheese," as the personification of the English settler. The *Oxford English Dictionary* indicates a British use of "Yankee" or "Yankey" as a surname from the Dutch, used in English as early as 1683 and applied in contempt to New Englanders by British soldiers. In fact, the earliest use in print was by the British commander James Wolfe, who wrote in a 1758 letter to another leader that "My posts are now so fortified that I can afford you two companies of Yankees, and the more as they are better for ranging and scouting than either work or vigilance." In case that wording did not already make clear his disdain for the Yankee soldier, Wolfe added this cold commentary: "The Americans are in general the dirtiest most contemptible cowardly dogs that you can conceive. There is no depending on them in action. They fall down dead in their own dirt and desert by battalions, offi-

cers and all. Such rascals as those are rather an encumber-
ance than any real strength to an army."

Three decades after Wolfe's initial impression, another visitor reported the continuing contempt implied by the term in
1784: "The New Englanders are disliked by the inhabitants
of all the other provinces, by whom they are called Yankeys,
by way of derision." Another stranger in America reported a
more respectable attitude, even a reverence, toward the term
in 1807: "This is so far from being considered a term of re-
proach by the inhabitants of New England, that it is employed
by them in the same manner, and perhaps with greater complacency, than a native of Old England applies to his countrymen the appellation of 'John Bull.'" Often preceded by
epithets (as in the title of the 1955 Broadway musical *Damn
Yankees,* about baseball), the term was extended by the turn
of the nineteenth century to Americans in general.

During the Civil War, though, "Yankee" became again a
term for a Northerner. In Margaret Mitchell's 1936 novel,
Gone With the Wind, Rhett Butler gave the term a back-
handed compliment in describing Northerners to Scarlett
O'Hara. "The Yankees aren't fiends," Rhett told her. "They
haven't horns and hoofs, as you seem to think. They are
pretty much like Southerners—except with worse manners,
of course, and terrible accents."

Even the term YANKEEISM has seen extension. From the
late eighteenth century, the noun has meant "a peculiarity or
trait that characterizes a Yankee"; as recently as 1946, a
Boston newspaper editorialized that "It is high time we in
New England stopped trafficking in the myth of Yankeeism."
Since 1806, however, the same noun has stood for "any word
or phrase typical of Yankee speaking"—TWISTICAL, for instance, as an adjective meaning "crooked or untrustwor-
thy"—and by further extension that noun has come to be
equated by enterprising speakers with AMERICANISM.

CHAPTER 9

DIRECTNESS

"All systems go," John A. Powers boomed into his microphone, heralding the early success of America's efforts to explore outer space. "Everything is A-OK."

When the space program was just getting started, Shorty Powers was its voice to the American people. He served as its public information officer, and by using sentence fragments ("All systems go") and forceful letters ("A-OK") that came from NASA engineers in the late 1950s, he quickly and confidently reassured the public about the continuing success of Project Mercury.

Such bluntness is nothing new for American workers. A century ago, the rules were spelled out exactly by a West Virginia board of education: "The Board don't want any teacher who cannot make their own fires, sweep School House, and chop their own wood free of charge." The top pay for a teacher willing to accept those conditions in 1897 was a monthly salary of $26.

Around the country, directness of expression takes many forms. In a 1985 autobiography, the Czech-born tennis player

Martina Navratilova noted a few of those forms. "Being blunt with your feelings is very American," she wrote. "In this big country, I can be as brash as New York, as hedonistic as Los Angeles, as sensuous as San Francisco, as brainy as Boston, as proper as Philadelphia, as bracing as Chicago, as warm as Palm Springs. . . ."

As a result of such bluntness, Americans can be fast talkers. Just as communications have quickened, so have the words being expressed. The directness of American cant can be seen in the eliminating of unnecessary words and the substituting of letters for words. This clipped language, nowhere more evident than in the parlance of modern technology, has roots dating back to colonial times. From express mail to E-mail, the communication of America has long depended on the power of directness.

LETTER FOR LETTER

America's affection for abbreviations is nothing new, stretching back to colonial days and ahead to tomorrow's technology. "E-mail" itself, for example, shortens the word "electronic" to its first letter, and its users tend to reduce entire phrases into clusters of letters, from BTW ("By the way") to IMHO ("In my humble opinion") and even AFAIK ("As far as I know").

Short terms in the American language tend to take the form of abbreviations (as in the three letters "H.E.W." for "Health, Education, and Welfare") or acronyms ("HUD" for "Housing and Urban Development"). The primary difference is one of pronunciation; abbreviations—often called "initialisms" by linguists—tend to be pronounced as separate letters, while an acronym, formed from the initial letters or sounds of a series of words, may be pronounced as a word or a wordlike name. By the randomness of American pronunciation, "S.A.T." is an abbreviation, its three letters pronounced separately and nowadays standing for "Scholastic Aptitude Test," but the medical test "CAT scan" has its first syllable pronounced like "cat" with the acronym's letters standing for "Computerized Axial Tomography."

Single letters as abbreviations have long stood for sins. Nathaniel Hawthorne, in his 1850 novel *The Scarlet Letter,* illustrated the wearing of the letter *A* for the crime of adultery. "Lastly . . . came back the rude market-place of the Puritan settlement," Hawthorne wrote, "with all the townspeople assembled and levelling their stern regards at Hester Prynne,— yes, at herself,—who stood on the scaffold of the pillory, an infant on her arm, and the letter A, in scarlet, fantastically embroidered with gold thread, upon her bosom!"

That alphabetical punishment was available in Massachusetts from the early days of the New England colonies until almost the end of the eighteenth century. In the initials of this symbolic branding, *B* stood for blasphemy, *D* for drunkenness, and *I* for incest. (According to *Our Own Words,* by Mary Helen Dohan, that last letter was already in use for identifying incest, so instead "the figure of an Indian cut out of red cloth was, like Hester Prynne's *A,* a brand of shame among the Puritans, marking the woman 'suffering an Indian to have carnal knowledge of her.' ") Not all letters used for dishonorable badges offered a clear indication of the crime. A 1947 history, for instance, indicated that " 'T' marks a thief," but the letter *V* could represent "those guilty of vulgarity or viciousness." That *V* was also suggested to represent "venery," the medieval term for sexual pleasure.

Modern American euphemism, oddly enough, has returned somewhat to the colonial practice, although today's euphemistic letters frequently stand for practices less immoral than those condemned by the colonists. Senator Gary Hart was asked in the 1980s about adultery, known then as the A-QUESTION, and baby talk has long alluded to the F-WORD among other obscenities. In the last decade, however, innocent euphemizing has become common, including the T-WORD (for "taxes") and, in a 1997 television commercial, the M-WORD (meaning "marriage").

CLIP JOINT

Perhaps the most direct and widely recognized of all American abbreviations is the ubiquitous "O.K." The history of that two-letter term of approval was long shrouded in mystery, until the word scholar Allen Walker Read tracked the term to its origins. Various theories of that abbreviation abounded. Some thought, for instance, that it came from an Indian term spelled *okeh,* while others pointed to "Aux Cayes" on shipments of rum through Haiti. More persuasive was the argument favoring an abbreviation of "Old Kinderhook," a nickname for Martin Van Buren; the eighth president had been born in Kinderhook, New York, and an 1840 organization of Democrats who supported him took the name of "the O.K. Club."

None of these theories, however, proved true. Through meticulous research, Professor Read was able to track the initials back to 1839, a year before the formation of the O.K. Club. The term first appeared as an abbreviation of the phrase "oll korrect," a humorous spelling of "all correct" used by newspaper editors in Boston. Although Andrew Jackson was accused of being barely literate and having originated the misspelling of that phrase, that assertion has been conclusively disproven.

And despite its worldwide acceptance, "O.K." has hardly been alone among the abbreviations in America. "U.S." itself came into the language soon after the country's founding. In 1791, George Washington warned, "A great quantity of bonds, thrown suddenly into the market, . . . could not but have effects the most injurious to the credit of the U.S." That abbreviation is now often found with numbers in the designation of interstate roads, such as "U.S. 1" along the East Coast. The longer abbreviation for "United States of America," as well as of "United States Army," is the three-letter "U.S.A." A headline in the *Pittsburgh Gazette* as early as 1795 referred to the "U.S.A. Congress," and the abbreviation enjoyed musical prominence in the 1985 Bruce Springsteen song "Born in the U.S.A." Much like "United States," that set of three initials has also been used to indicate the American language itself; during the First World War, a novelist had a British character sound disdainful of "Speakin' U.S.A., tommyrot!"

The earliest abbreviation for the new country has been much less successful over the centuries. "U. STATES" appeared in a 1787 government document's resolution "that the U. States in Congs. be authorized to elect a federal Executive." A Boston newspaper in 1832 referred to "the U. States Bank," and a New York publication in 1897 spoke of "a treaty with Nicaragua for the construction of an isthmian canal under the control of the U. States government." Otherwise, "U. States" has been overlooked as a clipped form, nor has anybody tried to initiate "United S." into the argot of abbreviations.

ALPHABET SOUP

Some American abbreviations, however, are not instantly recognizable in their attempts at directness. In fact, during the 1930s, the overuse of such terms as "T.V.A." (for "Tennessee Valley Authority") and "N.R.A." (then "National Recovery Administration" and now used by the National Rifle Association) caused criticism of the government's ALPHABET AGENCIES. Other abbreviations from American history have also led to confusion or uncertainty.

In 1839, the same year as the introduction of "O.K.," the

initials "N.G." came into print for an abbreviation of "no good" or "no go." A New Orleans newspaper reported on a romantic competition in 1839 that "Though his grey-headed rival tried to win, it was n.g. (no go!)." A generation later, "G.B." was the abbreviation for workers to fear. It stood for "grand bounce," based on an 1873 verb use of BOUNCE for "to dismiss or discharge," and an 1880 newspaper reported this exchange:

> "Well, I've got the g.b."
> "The geebee, Thomas! What in the nation is that?"
> "I've got the grand bounce—g.b. . . . I've been fired!"

John Bartlett's dictionary provided a definition of that phrase in 1877: "To get the grand bounce is to be dismissed from service; particularly from an office under government."

Just as a word's meaning may alter, an abbreviation's sense may change, and the same set of letters will move from one profession to another. Today the medical use of "O.R." stands for "operating room," the place for performing surgeries. That same set of initials, however, once was used as a legal term for "ordered recorded." Minutes taken from court records of 1790 reported that a transfer of "power of attorney from Alex Dever to Joseph McElurath is duly acknowledged & O.R." That lettering is now obsolete legalese but standard in medical terminology.

Other combinations of initials have come and gone in the American language. "T.T.T.," for example, is an obsolete abbreviation that was once familiar to drinkers. An 1841 report used the triple letters and stated that "They have temperance wagons in the West, marked with three Ts, to denote that the owner is a Tee-To-Taller." (From 1834 on, TEETOTAL was an emphatic way to proclaim total abstinence from alcohol, as if to indicate "TOTAL with a capital T.") The Underground Railroad was also known by the letters "U.G.R.R.," as in the wry headline of a Virginia newspaper during the Civil War: "Our 'Local' Visits Lincolndom—A Trip to Baltimore and Back by the 'U.G.R.R.' "

As the new country was being settled, the original settlers sometimes gained prestige for being an "F.F.," or "First Family." From those initials came "F.F.V.," a nineteenth-century shortening of "First Families of (or 'in') Virginia," a generation before "F.F.T." stood for "First Families of Tennessee." In 1840, "O.F.M." was used for "Our First Men," although no evidence for "O.F.W.," or "Our First Women," has been discovered. Student slang added the admirable abbreviation "B.M.O.C." during the past century, but that 1934 designation of "Big Man on Campus" is rarely heard these days.

The letters "G.T.T." came into English in 1839; twenty-five years later, an American observer commented, "Whenever, at one period, a smart Yankee failed in his business or expectations, he made himself scarce in his ancient locality, leaving behind him only the mystical letters 'G.T.T.' " Now historical, that abbreviation suggested a departure more enduring than when "Gone Fishing" is posted on an office door; the three letters stood for "Gone to Texas."

During World War I, the abbreviation "G.T.H." provided a euphemism for "Go to Hell," just as "G.B.F.," as a forerunner of today's "T.G.I.F.," euphemized the mantra of teachers: "God Bless Friday!"

Still familiar is the political abbreviation "G.O.P." for the Republican Party. Known after the Civil War as the "Grand Old Party" or the "Gallant Old Party," the Republican Party gained its lasting initials in the 1880s (although "grand old party" was used earlier for the Democratic Party). In this century, Harry Truman derided the Republican initials as standing for "Grand Old Platitudes."

Directness

A LITTLE SHORT

Directness has led not only to the abbreviation but also to the clipping of American words.

What appears to be an abbreviation, for instance, is not always so. Another nineteenth-century term, V SPOT, bears no relation to the G SPOT (or "Grätenberg spot") sought by sex researchers during the last generation. Instead, the *V* in that expression represents the Roman numeral for five, making "V spot" a five-dollar bill. Latinate initials also named the ten-dollar bill an *X,* and the twenty an *XX. The New Yorker* observed in 1837 that "The possession of a 'V' was a subject matter for rejoicing." Almost a century later, gamblers began to use *G* or GEE for a thousand dollars, an abbreviation for "grand." The stripper's G-STRING, of unknown origin, dates back to the 1870s, and G SUIT (from "gravity suit") for an astronaut's attire began in 1944.

Abbreviations also led to new words, such as "okay" in the 1840s from spelling out the pronunciation of "O.K." Back at the beginning of the 1800s, residents of Philadelphia enjoyed a special cake known as the APEE. That word was created by a baker named Ann Page. As a Pennsylvania history reported in 1830, "On her cakes she impressed the letters A.P., the letters of her name," leading to "apee" spelled out for the cake itself.

Shortened or clipped words date back to colonial usage. In 1704, Queen Anne offered a proclamation to determine the value of colonial money. The term for that colonial currency was PROCLAMATION MONEY, a name also applied by some states to their printing of paper bills during or after the Revolutionary War. A 1775 resolution, for example, called for the power "to collect Proclamation money to meet expenses incurred by delegates to the Continental Congress." As early as 1751, the word "money" was dropped from the term, leaving only "proclamation"; a New Jersey record showed the current rate of paying "Proclamation, for every 100 Acres."

Even shorter was the clipped PROC, an obsolete syllable in use since 1755, when a correspondent complained that "The Money I get since the Presidents Currency came out is all proc." The British-based currency valued by Queen Anne was described by a Virginia numismatist in 1860: "This money was called proc (i.e., proclamation money) and was issued on bits of thick paper, about the size of a playing card, and for various sums, from sixpence up to forty shillings."

Unrelated to this proc is a nineteenth-century homophone PROCK, a fanciful animal with four legs—two short legs opposite to the longer legs—allowing the animal to stand and graze on hillsides. Mentioned in an 1840 New Orleans newspaper, the quadruped was described in an 1896 publication as "that fabulous 'Prock,' an animal whose two right legs were only half the length of the left legs." The animal took on various other names, some as fanciful as the creature itself. A Michigan history in 1947 recounted that "Fierce animals invented to frighten greenhorns like the 'sidehill gouger' and the 'huija,' combine prankster and tall humor." The folklorist B. A. Botkin offered another variant of the name, SIDEHILL DODGER, along with this depiction of its living habits: "It lived on the sides of hills only. It had two short legs on the up-hill side. It burrowed in hillsides, having a number of such burrows and was always dodging in and out of these." In 1849, a rural letter writer was responsible for another version of this creature's name, the SIDEHILL CRITTER.

Students were responsible in the nineteenth century for the creation of PROF as a clipped form of "professor." This slang shortening appeared in a Yale magazine in 1838. In a rhyme about preparing examinations, the abbreviation led off a salute "For Proffs and Tutors too, / Who steer our big canoe." GRAD became the clipping of "graduate" in 1893, and within four years a former graduate was known as an OLD GRAD. The college president was known as PREX since 1828, and a few decades later became the PREXY. Similarly, the verb "substantiate" took on the shortened slang form of SUBSTANCHE. An 1838 newspaper reported a suspect's story: "He said he was only fending off the blows of her darned old rollin' pin, that she could substanche." Americans also shortened the British "promenade dance" to the still-popular PROM, which first appeared in an 1894 publication: "For two days . . . in January the room is crowded with 'Prom' girls and their escorts."

Although usually a word's ending was clipped, sometimes the beginning would be deleted. 'LASSES, for instance, dates back to Revolutionary times as a short form for "molasses." A broadside verse, printed on a large single sheet in 1775, criticized overindulgence: "The 'lasses they eat every day, / Would keep an house a winter." *The Chicago Tribune* still used the clipping as recently as 1948 to report that "Now, come spring, it's 'lasses time' right over the border and 'sap's a-bilin'.'" In 1807, Washington Irving first cut "molasses candy" to 'LASSES CANDY. During the 1980s, modern teenage slang took a similar turn, using such front-clipped terms as ZA for "pizza" and RENTS for "parents." The pattern continued in the 1990s, with ZINE being used for "online magazine."

FASTER TALK

The Civil War, a time in our country's history that called for directness and vigorous action, saw a vogue of shortened words come into the language.

MILISH was an 1862 compression of the noun "militia." Similarly, "position" led to the shorter POSISH. That colloquialism appeared in an 1862 military comment about naval strategy: "Snorting their impatience to 'get into posish,' came the *Monitor,* the *Galena* and others." The colloquial SECESH (a shortening of the noun "secession," for the withdrawal of Southern states from the Union) was used as both noun and verb. Northerners applied the term to any Confederate, as in an 1861 army letter that related the story of a disturbance in a Union camp. Alarmed about the possibility of finding Southern soldiers nearby, Union scouts investigated a loud noise and, according to the correspondent, "The guards soon found the secesh to be a great hog that was wandering round in the woods." The verb, an unusual variant for "secede," also turned up in 1861 as part of a record of the rebellion: "He has plenty of money, which I find is a good thing to secesh with."

By 1865, the clipped OSOPHY, as in "philosophy" or "theosophy," began to be used, sometimes facetiously. An American's evaluation of the British Hampton Court called it "a parliament in which the idiosyncracies, isms and osophies of race and nation . . . are represented in a pleasant and instructive manner." In 1897, a philosopher noted, "That man would be hard to please who could not find . . . some variety of doxy, or osophy, or ism, which would come within hailing distance of his theory of life and destiny."

Perhaps the most successful of the Civil War clipped words came from the American jurist Oliver Wendell Holmes Jr., who reduced "business" to BIZ. In an 1861 quotation, Holmes commented on a work week that "has been the first that really looked like biz." A British shortening, BUS, was pronounced the same and was applied in the theater of the 1860s to any action or business onstage. It was not, however, until the end of World War II that the American shortening became widespread in the phrase SHOW BIZ, and by the mid-1970s the expression THAT'S SHOW BIZ! was a cliché to communicate resignation or an indication of defeat.

Among the most important clippings of the twentieth century is GAS. Out of the 1779 noun "gas," for matter that is not liquid or solid, came the 1865 noun "gasoline" for liquid fuel.

After the turn of the century, "gasoline" was cut back to "gas," and World War I introduced such slang expressions as OUT OF GAS for slowing or stopping and STEP ON THE GAS for increasing speed.

The search for speedier communication has been a continuing obsession with the American public. EXPRESS MAIL, for instance, dates back almost two centuries in the United States, although its original meaning was far from the "overnight delivery" that modern correspondents have come to expect. In fact, here is an 1813 announcement of the system promising prompt service: "An express mail is established between Washington and Buffalo, N. Y., to arrive in 4 days 18 hours." The western version of such service led to the PONY EXPRESS, but that rapid relay of ponies operated for only sixteen months, on a route between St. Joseph, Missouri, and Sacramento, California. Before that route was established, the term was already current in the language. A New York newspaper on December 18, 1847, reminded its readers about the speed of news, noting, "By our pony express from the South, we have intelligence from New Orleans to the afternoon of the 2d." When the actual service appeared in 1860, an advertisement for riders suggested the danger inherent in its efforts to speed the mail: "Wanted—young, skinny, wiry fellows, not over eighteen. Must be expert riders, willing to risk death daily. Orphans preferred."

Today's first-class mail, generally faster than in the nineteenth century, has taken as its slang name the rhyming SNAIL MAIL. In contrast, the abbreviated E-MAIL first appeared in the early 1980s for a shortening of "electronic mail," transmitted by Internet.

As the result of the speeding up of technology, older Americans may well sympathize with Mr. Wilson in "Dennis the Menace." As the comic strip's gruff elderly neighbor watches young Dennis at a computer keyboard, he marvels: "We had tin-can phones. . . . He's got the World Wide Web!"

Web Words

WEBAHOLIC a person addicted to using the World Wide Web; a recent use of the combining form -HOLIC as in "alcoholic" and "chocaholic"

WEBCAST a newscast delivered over the Web; a term on the analogy of "broadcast"

WEB CHAT conversation on the Internet; a noun phrase using "chat," from a Middle English verb related to "chatter"

WEBHEAD a frequent user of the Web; another use of the combining form -HEAD as in "deadhead" for a devoted fan of the Grateful Dead's music

WEB-MART commercial activity on the Web; a term based on a store name such as Kmart

WEBMERCIAL any commercial placed on the Web; a fusion on the analogy of the blend "infomercial"

WEB-SURFER one who tries various sites on the Web; a computer version of "channel surfer" for one who changes television channels frequently

WEB-VERTISING advertising on the Web, or the use of Webmercials; a blending of "World Wide Web" and "advertising"

WEB WARRIOR person who uses the Web; an alliterative phrase on the analogy of "weekend warrior"

WEBZINE a magazine found on the World Wide Web

CHAPTER 10

INDIRECTNESS

*H*ot and spicy, the controversy will long be remembered in Congress as the Great Chili Debate of 1974.

In the early months of that year, an extended argument began in the Senate about which state of the Union makes the finest bowl of chili. Before it ended, the argument included an assertion by Senator Barry Goldwater of Arizona that "a Texan does not know chili from leavings in a corral." Two days later, Senator Robert Taft Jr. of Ohio altered the euphemism from "leavings in a corral" to "barnyard apples."

As early as 1840, pioneers had their own term for recycled animal droppings, with dried frontier dung euphemistically known as BUFFALO CHIPS. In a much more recent column, the newspaper humorist Dave Barry placed quotation marks around a related euphemism: ACTS OF CONGRESS.

Indirectness in American speech has long taken the form of euphemism as well as the use of word inflation (as in "controlled flight into terrain" for an airplane crash) and code words (such as "traditional" for issues and ideas favored by conservatives). This strain in the development of American language, in direct contrast to the directness known by Harry Truman's supporters as "plain speaking," has allowed speakers and writers to allude to subjects that would not otherwise be discussed. Through euphemisms and code words, America's way of speaking has grown indirectly as well as directly.

ROUNDING OFF

The poet Emily Dickinson, who referred to herself with deprecating humor as "the belle of Amherst," played with language in indirect ways that still catch the imagination. In poems that resemble riddles, she described various natural and artificial phenomena without directly identifying the subjects of her works. "A narrow Fellow in the Grass" (Poem 986), for example, was her depiction (c. 1865) of a snake, inducing memorable feelings:

> But never met this Fellow
> Attended, or alone
> Without a tighter breathing
> And Zero at the Bone—

Even more roundabout was her poetic understanding of a train. "I like to see it lap the Miles," Dickinson wrote about the "iron horse" (an 1840 metaphor for the steam locomotive), "And lick the Valleys up— / And stop to feed itself at Tanks— . . ." (Poem 585).

Dickinson's wayward wording was not, however, immediately appreciated by other poets and critics. In fact, few of her works were published until decades after her death, and those poems she did allow to circulate received less than flattering commentary. "The rhymes were all wrong," one reader huffed, and the critical consensus during her lifetime was summed up in a dismissive sentence: "They are quite as remarkable for defects as for beauties and are generally devoid of true poetical qualities." Since the poet's death more than a century ago, the poems have seen the widespread publication and praise that eluded Dickinson throughout her lifetime.

Indirect wording has also been used with determination as a frequent form of communication in Congress. Prior to the Civil War, Senator Charles Sumner of Masschusetts vigorously denounced the proslavery forces in the United States Senate, and in an 1856 personal attack upon Senator Stephen Douglas of Illinois, Sumner resorted to indirect name-calling. "No person with the upright form of man," he began, his voice rising with fury, "can be allowed without the violation of all decency to switch out from his tongue the perpetual stench of offensive personality."

Turning directly to his adversary, he continued his attack on the Illinois speaker of ill-chosen words: "Sir, this is not a proper weapon of debate, at least, on this floor! The noisome, squat, and nameless animal to which I now refer is not a proper model for an American Senator. Will the Senator from Illinois take notice!" (Soon after the indirect "skunk" attack, Senator Sumner was physically attacked by a southern congressman, Preston Brooks of South Carolina, who brutally beat him with a cane.)

Such indirectness of language continues to apply. In 1984 Representative Barney Frank interrupted a speech with this parliamentary inquiry: "Is the term 'crybaby' an appropriate phrase to be used in a debate in the House?" Only rarely, though, has Congress become as exercised about the political ramifications of food as it did during its unsettling chili debate.

PARDON MY LANGUAGE

As a form of indirectness, euphemism in American history has long taken the form of meiosis, or deliberate understatement.

In 1773, American colonists protested British taxation by throwing overboard the tea on three ships in Boston Harbor; the historic episode became known as the "Boston Tea Party," and its participants took on the jocular identity of TEA SPILLERS. A member of the next generation exclaimed in 1837, "Certainly we sons of the tea-spillers are a marvellously patient generation!"

Similarly, the bloodiness of the American Civil War took on the euphemism of the LATE UNPLEASANTNESS, introduced by the humorist Petroleum V. Nasby; an 1868 edition of *The Congressional Globe* used that term, as well as a variant: "The rebel generals . . . think the 'little unpleasantness' did not amount to much, after all."

Nineteenth-century words, particularly in describing clothing and body parts, were often euphemistic. In 1859, the lexicographer John Bartlett defined HOSE in Ohio and points west as "the Western term for 'stockings,' which is considered extremely indelicate, although 'long socks' is pardonable." The twentieth-century use of UNMENTIONABLES for underwear was preceded by the carefulness of referring to trousers a century earlier as UNWHISPERABLES; an 1837 article in *Knickerbocker Magazine* included the subject's need to "see about procuring himself a new pair of unwhisperables from his host." By 1890, what the trousers covered could be referred to as SUBTROUSERS, as in a Columbus, Ohio, newspaper that reported the shocking indecency when "four inches of white canvass subtrousers was exposed." Following the Civil War, the phrase BLOODY SHIRT (waved as a symbol of the desire for vengeance against the South) was euphemized as "the ensanguined undergarment."

The body parts covered by those sensitively named clothes were also unmentionable, as the story of a British traveler in the nineteenth century revealed. After Captain Frederick Marryat visited America in 1839, he reported to his English readers that "There are certain words which are never used in America, but an absurd substitute is employed. . . . When at Niagara Falls I was escorting a young lady with whom I was on friendly terms. She had been standing on a piece of rock, the better to view the scene, when she slipped down, and was evidently hurt by the fall: she had, in fact, grazed her shin. As she limped a little in walking home, I said, 'Did you hurt your LEG much?' She turned from me, evidently much shocked, or much offended. . . . After some hesitation, she said that as she knew me well, she would tell me that the word leg was never mentioned before ladies." The young woman added that the preferred term was LIMB, adding, "I am not so particular as some people are, for I know those who always say limb of a table, or limb of a piano-forte." A decade after Marryat's faux pas, Henry Wadsworth Longfellow offered BENDER as a jocular alternative; the poet wrote, "Young ladies are not allowed to cross their benders in school."

Descriptions, particularly those thought to be unkind or negative when spoken plainly, required the inventing of euphemisms. Bartlett reported a New England phrase in 1859, HAVE ON HIGH-HEELED SHOES, as a term for haughtiness. "To say of a woman that she 'has on her high-heeled shoes,' " Bartlett wrote, "is to intimate that she sets herself up as a person of more consequence than others allow her to be; or in other words, that she is 'stuck up.' "

Those reluctant in the nineteenth century to describe the elderly through use of the straightforward "old" turned to the euphemism AGEABLE. A census taker reported in 1845 on "Judy Tompkins, ageable woman, and four children." More than a century later, the word had become part of American dialect when a southern writer commented, "My own daddy lived to be very ageable, but I don't know when he died." A more common phrase in current use is OF A CERTAIN AGE.

CODE NAME: WALKER

Mystery may be the result whenever America's wording has become too indirect or deliberately difficult.

Some names used as euphemisms, for instance, have become shrouded in historical mist. WALKER is such a name, heard during an 1882 visit to America, but the original Walker whose name was used as a verb remains unknown. " 'Hock my sparks,' 'soak my gems,' and 'Walker my diamonds,' " the traveler recalled, were at that time used as "American euphemisms for the act of pawning your jewellery," the origins unknown.

Easier to pinpoint is the source of the noun and verb TROLLOPE. The term dates back to Frances Milton Trollope, an Englishwoman whose writings of the early nineteenth century criticized the manners of Americans after she visited the United States. The noun form appeared by 1834 in a study of American manners: "Whenever an individual in a playhouse happens, when seated in the boxes, to turn his back towards the pit, or, occupying a front seat, to put his feet on the benches, (a want of decorum severely censured by Mrs. Trollope) a general outcry of 'Trollope, Trollope' is heard from every part of the house." An equivalent phrase today would be the generalized "Down in front!" for anybody blocking the view of others.

The same writer's name became a verb in an 1848 book review: "Travelers, male and female . . . come Trolloping over our country, to seek what blemishes they may descry." An earlier version of the verb was TROLLOPIZE, used in an 1834 edition of a New York newspaper observing that "The right honourable secretary of the colonial department, Mr. Stanley, has been Trollopized." ("Trollope" itself is a habitation name, from a place meaning "troll's hollow," and is not directly related to the 1621 use of "trollop" for a promiscuous woman.)

A more insidious way to disguise meaning can be the use of

unfamiliar names and terms. These expressions often are formed of Greek and Latin roots that require deciphering in order to understand the hidden meanings. Human fears are especially susceptible to encoding into difficult vocabulary. Hundreds of such phobias have been identified in recent decades, with the writers of dictionaries at a disadvantage to keep up with the neologisms. Following is a baker's dozen of these phobic formations:

ALGOPHOBIA a fear of pain or suffering

ATOMOSOPHOBIA a fear of atomic or nuclear explosions

AVIOPHOBIA a fear of flight or flying

BRONTOPHOBIA a fear of thunder and lightning

DEMOPHOBIA a fear of crowds or large groups

LYGOPHOBIA a fear of nighttime or darkness

METATHESIOPHOBIA a fear of changes

MYSOPHOBIA a fear of dirt or germs

OPHIDIOPHOBIA a fear of snakes

PANOPHOBIA a fear of everything

THANATOPHOBIA a fear of death or dying

TRAUMATOPHOBIA a fear of injury or being hurt

TRISKAIDEKAPHOBIA a fear of the number 13

SOFTLY SPOKEN

Indirectness is often employed in the American tongue, even when the soft wording is completely unnecessary. A judge on

American television, for instance, recently accused the defendant in a trial of offering "some C and B story."

Here the abbreviations are being substituted for words that might seem offensive to some: "cock" and "bull." That expression, however, was not intended to offend. The phrase COCK AND BULL STORY dates back almost four centuries in English usage, based most likely on a now-forgotten fable in which a rooster and a bull spoke to each other in fantastic terms. In the twentieth century, the unrelated COCKAMAMIE first appeared in American slang; sometimes spelled "cockamamy," it was an altering of "decalcomania," a Civil War–era term for transferring pictures from paper to glass, now more familiar in the clipped form of "decal."

Other practitioners of law and order as well as etiquette have resorted to frequent uses of euphemism. Vigilante justice in the Old West, for example, took on the euphemism of REGULATING COMPANY. An 1828 letter from the West, referring to physical force as a "strong arm," informed readers that "When a horse thief, a counterfeiter, or any other desperate vagabond, infested a neighborhood, evading justice by cunning, or by a strong arm, . . . the citizens formed themselves into a 'regulating company,' a kind of holy brotherhood, whose duty was to purge the community of its unruly members."

In the late nineteenth century, the elegance of euphemism was used in attempts to sidestep justice. An 1871 report concluded, "The man of violence, who had heretofore been denounced as a murderer, now appeared before the charitable jury as a modest STABBIST, or, at worst, called a formidable STRIKIST."

Sometimes a euphemism has taken on the sinister sense of a CODE WORD. That 1884 expression, designating a term with a secret meaning, applies to any phrase that seems innocuous but attempts to communicate a hidden sense. This type of euphemism is exemplified by the 1966 phrase "family values," used as a Republican attack term during the 1992 presidential campaign; ostensibly meant to support the moral values of the nuclear family unit, the words became perceived by some as shorthand for intolerance of homosexual rights and abortion.

Today's euphemisms tend to inflate single words into elaborate phrases. "Old" has been replaced by "semi-antique," "used" by "previously owned." The simple "coupon" has been enlarged by newspaper advertisements into "gift certificate," while products that were once "on sale" are now "promotionally priced." Wrinkles are referred to as "face rhytides," libraries have become "media arts centers," a personal trainer is known as an "exercise physiologist," and prostitutes nowadays are often called "sex workers."

Ever-vigilant critics of offensive language, however, may go too far in protecting the decency of American English. For instance, the National Highway Traffic Safety Administration, which studies traffic accidents, has decided to eliminate the word "accident" in favor of "crash"; the report previously known as the Fatal Accident Reporting System became known in 1996 as the Fatal Analysis Reporting System, with a public awareness campaign titled "Crashes Aren't Accidents."

WAR IS HECK

War is probably the strongest catalyst for the formation of euphemisms as examples of indirect wording.

In recent years, military euphemisms for death have included "casualty," "collateral damage," and "incident." When President Bill Clinton chose to deploy American troops in Bosnia in 1995, he warned the public that "no deployment of American troops is risk free, and this one may well involve casualties. There may be accidents in the field or incidents with people who have not given up their hatred."

The lexicographer Hugh Rawson explains the popularity of these formations as a way to sidestep blunter or stronger wording. Rawson's *Dictionary of Euphemisms* identifies "incident" as "a generalized term, whose value for covering up crisis, catastrophe, disaster, etc., has received worldwide recognition. For example, the Japanese referred to the war that they started with China on July 7, 1937, as 'the China incident.' " Here is Rawson's list of related euphemisms: "ABERRATION, ABNORMAL OCCURRENCE, ACCIDENT, BROKEN ARROW, EPISODE, EVENT, INVOLVEMENT, IRREGULARITY, PROBLEM, SITUATION, and THING."

Even in the conflicts over animal rights, the American language has been adapted to euphemisms to avoid direct expressions about killing. Humane societies, for example, put out EUTHANIZE or PUT DOWN as the preferred term for the killing of unwanted animals, whether healthy or not. Activists in favor of sparing healthy pets despite their unwanted numbers have turned in the last decade to a philosophy known as NO-KILL, perhaps in analogy to the NO-FLY zones over Iraq, the NO-BAKE pie ingredients in grocery stores, or the NO-PAY loans that delay the accruing of interest in some financial transactions.

Perhaps the most confusing of American euphemisms is the phrase BUY THE FARM, which means "to die." Those uninitiated in the slang verb's meaning may think mistakenly that the deceased is still alive and purchasing property. In use among jet pilots by the early 1950s, this euphemism has various forms, including "buy the shop" as well as "buy the ranch" and "buy the back forty."

Famous Last Words

ETERNAL CAMPING GROUND a nineteenth-century westernism, perhaps based on the native use of "happy hunting ground" for the destination after death

GO FOR IT a verb phrase meaning "to die" and used in various forms since 1845

GONE UNDER an 1847 term, perhaps from an Indian expression, meaning "dead"

LAY AWAY an 1866 term for "to bury," first used in print by the poet John Greenleaf Whittier

GRAVEYARD COUGH an 1873 phrase for a fierce cough that indicates the approach of death

ON THE ICE Mark Twain's 1892 expression for preserving a corpse, leading to the use of "keep on ice" for reserving or being prepared

BUY ONE a World War I term from military aviation for "to be killed in air combat"

ENDSVILLE a 1961 noun for "death," often capitalized

BITE IT a 1960s phrase for "to be killed," perhaps based on the Homeric phrase "bite the dust" and leading to the more recent "bite the big one"

ACE a verb for "to murder" appearing in detective novels since 1975

A 1955 issue of *American Speech* defined the term as originating in fatal air crashes, explaining, "Jet pilots say that when a jet crashes on a farm the farmer usually sues the government for damages done to his farm by the crash, and the amount demanded is always more than enough to pay off the mortgage and then buy the farm outright. Since this type of crash is nearly always fatal to the pilot, the pilot pays for the farm with his life."

An earlier term is the ultimate western euphemism for death, which is the lighthearted BOOT HILL (or BOOTS HILL). It was popularized along with BOOT GRAVEYARD, explained by a western writer in an 1881 essay on Dodge City, the Kansas outpost of frontier civilization: "There is at this place a yard called the Boot Grave-yard, a place well known to all western men, and called thus from the fact that thirty-eight men have been buried there with their boots on." An 1877 work on Dodge City placed the name "Boot Hill" into quotation marks, and from that term came the widespread designation of any cemetery or graveyard for those killed violently, usually gunned down or hanged.

Based upon that euphemism is the name of Florida's Boot Hill Saloon, a popular bar situated across from the Daytona Beach town cemetery and advertised with a clever couplet:

Order a drink and have a seat.
You're better off here than across the street.

In addition to Boot Hill, America's language has been enlivened by more than its share of euphemisms for death and expiring. Consider the generous coupon offered by a Virginia tobacco shop. Offering special values to those who buy in quantity, the coupon adds that it "expires when you do."

Emotionally Speaking

The American Heart

CHAPTER 11

PRIDE

Abraham Lincoln labored to express his hyperbolic pride in the United States two dozen years before the Civil War. "All the armies of Europe, Asia and Africa combined," Lincoln announced in an 1837 speech in Illinois, "with all the treasure of the earth (our own excepted) in their military chest, with a Bonaparte for a commander, could not by force take a drink from the Ohio or make a track on the Blue Ridge in a trial of a thousand years."

Pride is not just an American trait. Also known as "superbia," pride forms the basis of all the deadly sins. In American usage, however, pride often displays itself in the language of politics and patriotism, and the expressions that result have the power to stir as well as to take a stand. The poet John Greenleaf Whittier expressed that power in a Civil War verse about Frederick, Maryland, and its most celebrated inhabitant:

> "Shoot, if you must, this old gray head,
> But spare your country's flag," she said.

Frederick, also the burial place for Francis Scott Key, who wrote the words to the National Anthem in 1814, was immortalized by the 1863 poem "Barbara Frietchie." The poet John Greenleaf Whittier set in verse this story of an elderly patriot, whose name is now often spelled Barbara *Fritchie,* after she faced down an enemy army and experienced a rare example of civility during the Civil War. At that time, the troops of Stonewall Jackson occupied Frederick. The defiant woman, who was over the age of ninety-five, waved her Union flag before the Confederate army, but General Jackson interceded on her behalf. Whittier reports Jackson's response:

"Who touches a hair of yon gray head
Dies like a dog! March on!" he said.

Fritchie's story, still celebrated in Frederick, typifies the pride in patriotism that has marked America's words and ways over the centuries.

FEDERAL CASE

In terms of political pride, few statements have exceeded the sentiment expressed by George Washington in his famed Farewell Address of September 19, 1796. "The name of American," he told his fellow Americans, "which belongs to you in your national capacity, must always exalt the just pride of patriotism more than any appellation derived from local discriminations."

Common terms in modern politics, including "Democrat" and "government in action," have not always been similarly celebrated. The historians Charles and Mary Beard observed in 1939 that "At no time . . . had the American people officially proclaimed the United States to be a democracy. The Constitution did not contain the word or any word lending countenance to it, except possibly the mention of 'We, the people,' in the preamble. . . . When the Constitution was framed no respectable person called himself or herself a democrat." Another phrase that lacks overwhelming support has been "government in action," which, according to political pessimists, is a contradiction in terms (political wags often point to "military intelligence" as a similar oxymoron).

Rarely does the federal government receive credit for quick thinking or rapid reaction to the people's needs. In fact, the legendary slowness of federal aid dates back at least to the days of ratifying the Constitution, and the name that became synonymous back then with the slowness of governmental action was that of AMY DARDIN.

Mrs. Dardin was a Virginia widow who wanted Congress to compensate her for a horse pressed into army use during the Revolutionary War. In 1796, her claim first came before Congress, but no money was provided. At regular intervals, the claim was repeated, Congress after Congress, until after the War of 1812. By the time the woman died without restitution from the 1815 Congress, "Amy Dardin" had become familiar as a term for political procrastination. Davy Crockett wrote of settling another case in 1835, pointing out that settlement would be "better than hanging on like Amy Dardin for fifty years; and then get pay for a horse pressed during the Revolution; and indeed this case of Amy Dardin shew much of the course of proceeding."

BLUE LAWS

Early British put-downs of the American language seemed to focus on terms of pride and politics. An 1809 attack upon the Americanisms in Noah Webster's dictionary pointed out that "CONGRESSIONAL, PRESIDENTIAL and DEPARTMENTAL are barbarisms, in common use, we allow; but one of the same class, GOVERNMENTAL, which is equally worthless, is omitted." That unlisted adjective did appear as early as 1744 in Georgia, though, and the reason for Webster's failure to include it remains unclear.

In addition to procrastination, early government in America was also attacked for the development of laws based upon the strict puritanical regulations once enforced in New England. The Reverend Samuel A. Peters, a loyalist who fled the country in 1774, was first to use the expression BLUE LAW, but the origins of the term remain obscure. Some historians have suggested that the term came from the practice in New Haven of binding domestic laws into a blue cover. A second theory points to the British use of "blue" for the disapproving Presbyterians who condemned the licentiousness of the Restoration under Charles II and chose blue as their color to contrast with the royal red; proponents of this theory note that the similarly disapproving Puritans may well have caused this use of "blue" to cross the Atlantic and be applied to laws for strict moral conduct.

"Blue law" began as a term for New Haven regulations. Reverend Peters offered another prominent theory when he commented in a 1781 history of Connecticut, later known as the "Blue Law State," that "Even the rigid fanatics of Boston, and the mad zealots of Hertford . . . christened them the Blue Laws" and that these "were very properly termed Blue Laws; i.e. bloody Laws; for they were all sanctified with . . . whippings, cutting off the ears, burning the tongue and death." A generation later came this example: "One of the blue laws of Connecticut was, neither to give meat, drink, or lodging to a Quaker, or to tell him the road." Later historians, however, have dismissed many of these supposed laws as works of the imagination or, in Mitford Mathews's term, "splenetic fabrications."

Definitely borrowed from Britain, however, was the governing use of the phrase WARN OUT, meaning "to serve official notice that a person must leave town." The expression, already in use in England, was recorded in Deerfield, Massachusetts, in a 1758 vote "that the Selectmen be directed to warn the two children of Margaret Choulton out of Town Immediately." Twelve years later, another historical note shows that such a warning did not always prove permanent, as a Moses McEntosh "was warned out of Boston abote 17 years ago" and now was again being "warned in his Majesty's name to Depart this town of Boston in 14 Days."

The dismissal from town was not meant merely as a means to reduce the number of local criminals; this warning out could also relieve a township from responsibility to care for its destitute, and those who were given such a notice did not necessarily leave. A New England historian commented in 1911, "The effect of warning out as thus practiced upon persons who remained in the town after being warned was to relieve the town from all obligation to aid them if they became poor and in need of help or support."

POLITICAL PRIDE

America's proudest politicians have long suffered from ailments of varied names in their quests for more power. POTOMAC FEVER, named for the Potomac River which flows through Washington, was identified by Harry Truman in his memoirs: " 'Potomac fever,' too, creates a great desire on the part of people to see their names in print." Other modern pains in politics include HILL FEVER, for those seeking power in Congress on Capitol Hill, as well as a PRESIDENTIAL BUG supposedly carrying PRESIDENTIAL FEVER.

That fever was first identified in print in 1882 and was explained a generation later in a study of American government:

"Presidential fever, a phrase used to denote the eager desire for, and ambition to gain, the presidency of the United States, prevalent among prominent political leaders and 'favorite sons' in the several states." (Not part of this array of illnesses is WASHINGTON INFLUENZA. That sickness was identified more than a century ago in an account of George Washington's struggles during the Revolutionary War: "From some mismanagement Washington was detained at the Roxbury line nearly two hours, and exposed to a raw northeast wind, by which exposure he took a severe cold. Many others were similarly affected, and so general was the distemper that it was called the 'Washington Influenza.' ")

The presidential bug, according to *Safire's New Political Dictionary,* may have come from a story told by Abraham Lincoln about a "chin fly." Lincoln's story, related to a *New York Times* editor, made a point about Treasury Secretary Salmon P. Chase, who may have himself felt the bite of that power-hungry bug and wanted Lincoln's job. The president began his farm story by recalling: "My brother and I . . . were once plowing corn on a Kentucky farm, I was driving the horse, and he holding the plough. The horse was lazy but on one occasion rushed across the field so that I, with my long legs, could scarcely keep pace with him. On reaching the end of the furrow, I found an enormous chin fly fastened upon him, and knocked him off. My brother asked me what I did that for. I told him I didn't want the old horse bitten in that way. 'Why,' said my brother, 'that's all that made him go!' Now if Mr. C[hase] has a presidential chin fly biting him, I'm not going to knock him off, if it will only make his department go."

Beyond a candidate's presidential bug was the public's growing interest in that candidate, leading to a PRESIDENTIAL BOOM. Experienced by the proud electorate, this feeling of exhilaration about the leading candidate was initially identified in 1887. The boom could also be suppressed, though; in an

1892 edition of the *Chicago Tribune,* the editors dismissed one contender with "Holman's presidential boom may be likened to a gob of dough that hasn't a bit of yeast within a thousand miles of it."

If the successful candidate for the office proved less than capable, Thomas Jefferson called for AMOVABILITY, or the political power to remove that person from office. Jefferson wrote in 1816, seven years after ending his presidency, "Let us retain amovability on the concurrence of the executive and legislative branches."

Most shameful was the failure to vote for any candidate, which led to the derogatory designation of VOTE-DODGER, analogous to the "draft dodger" who avoids military service when called. In 1852, a Minnesota writer derogated one candidate as "a wily sort of politician in Indian tactics, it seems, like some of our own vote-dodgers." The noun was probably based on the earlier verb phrase TO DODGE A VOTE. *The Congressional Globe* in 1846 carried a vehement denial "that I dodged the vote," a denouncement of political dirty tricks issued by an accused evader.

Patriotic pride, on the other hand, led to the coining of OLD GLORY, used since the Civil War to refer to the American flag.

Old Glory

OLD TENOR "old money," or a 1730s term for currency from before a new currency was introduced at a different valuation

OLD DOMINION a 1770s term for the state of Virginia, previously known as the "ancient Dominion"

OLD CONGRESS the Congress under the Articles of Confederation; a term already in use by 1789 for the government before the Constitution was adopted

OLD FIELD SCHOOL a country elementary school set in a field that was formerly cultivated; the Weems biography of Washington in 1806 stated, "The first place of education to which George was ever sent, was a little 'old field school' "

OLD COLONY the Plymouth colony; an 1809 term, now historical, for the oldest New England settlement

OLD COUNTRYMAN a New World term used in 1828 to refer to a visiting Englishman; according to Bartlett's 1848 definition, the phrase referred only to visitors from Great Britain and was "never applied to persons from the Continent of Europe"

OLD THIRTEEN an 1840s reference to the thirteen original colonies that fought the American Revolution

OLD TIMEY an 1850 adjective to describe qualities or situations of an earlier generation

OLD PROBABILITIES a nickname for America's first weatherman, originally used in the 1870s and soon shortened to "old Probs"

OLD MAN a Native American usage for "wise man or seer," recorded in a 1903 history: "Certain individuals gain a remarkable . . . respect for wisdom or hunting skill. . . . These men are the so-called 'old-men' often mentioned in Indian manifestoes"

VOICE VOTE

America's pride in its political vocabulary stems at least partly from eponyms—proper names that become words with meanings in their own right—and even the names may be inventions.

ROORBACK, for instance, refers to any lie made public for political gain. It came from the name of a fictional character, a Baron von Roorback, who supposedly traveled throughout America and published a record of his journeys. This publication contained an implication that James Knox Polk, struggling to win the presidency in 1844, had owned and sold slaves. Immediately, "Roorback" became the term for any political canard, and by 1848, a Kentucky newspaper was using the term as a verb: "Whiggery was galvanized into renewed life by discovering that there was two lives of General Cass about, differing a bit from each other, and could not help Roorbacking over the discovery."

Sometimes the American eponymy developed from the name of somebody otherwise obscure in history. RUCKERIZE is a nineteenth-century verb formed from the name "Rucker"; during the national convention in Baltimore of 1836, no representative from Tennessee was present to cast that state's votes, and a citizen of Tennessee named E. Rucker, who happened to be attending the convention, was called upon to substitute. Twenty years later, when the episode was recounted, the historian acknowledged that "This latitudinarian proceeding gave rise to the phrase 'Ruckerize,' which was then and afterwards used to describe that and other similar contrivances."

Often, though, the name that added a term to the American language was that of a political figure seeking notoriety. Elbridge Gerry was a distinguished politician in early-nineteenth-century Massachusetts when the Democratic and Federal parties were vying for control of that state. Gerry designed a plan that would redistrict the voting divisions of the northeastern area to limit much of the Federal vote to one district. Retellings of the story have added apocryphal details, some suggesting that the painter Gilbert Stuart added lines to Gerry's map to form a head and a tail of a creature that he proclaimed a salamander, causing a Boston newspaper editor, Benjamin Russell, to reply: "Salamander? Call it a GERRY-MANDER!" The political term endured, although Gerry's name was pronounced with a hard G, whereas the eponym is now usually pronounced with a soft G. The source of the eponym is sometimes varied; after a 1961 plan to redistrict New York, Governor Nelson Rockefeller was accused of ROCKYMANDERING.

Another name in political history yielded the expression GOOD ENOUGH MORGAN. When William Morgan tried to publish a book in 1826 revealing the secrets of Masonry, the author disappeared just before its publication, and the Masons were charged with having taken him. From that disappearance came the term for any political scheme or plan to be used temporarily in getting votes. Thurlow Weed, a party leader at that time, reported an exchange challenging the Masons: " 'After we have proven that the body found at Oak Orchard is that of Timothy Monroe, what will you do for a Morgan?' . . . 'That is a good enough Morgan for us until you bring back the one you carried off.' " Almost a century later, *Collier's Magazine* included the phrase in a 1920 issue: "Anyway, it's a good-enough Morgan until after the election."

A place name can also establish a political eponym. ROW UP SALT RIVER, for example, refers to the ability to defeat a challenger, particularly in a political contest. SALT RIVER itself was used as early as 1659 for any river with a saltwater tide that comes almost to its source. By the nineteenth century, the phrase was used to describe anybody who was uncivilized or backwoodsy in speech. An 1835 essay indicated "a well-known rivalry between the collectors of the Downing dialect of New England, and the Crockett or Salt River dialect of the South and West." Perhaps the Salt River in Kentucky was the source, although a New York newspaper in 1910 pointed out the mystery of the term's source: "That imaginary stream called 'Salt River,' up which defeated candidates are supposed to be rowed, is one of the most felicitous of all our political Americanisms, although its authorship is unknown."

WEASEL WORDING

Not every user of America's growing vocabulary has expressed pride in the nation's political coinages.

In the early years of the twentieth century, TENNIS CABINET was lightly applied to the close circle around Theodore Roosevelt. A 1914 book on American government explained it as "a term applied by the newspaper press to the personal friends of President Roosevelt, some of whom played tennis with him, and with whom he was supposed to have had special confidential relations, even to the extent of conference on important public questions." This playful wording was probably based on the earlier KITCHEN CABINET, an alliterative phrase for the circle of friends who advised Andrew Jackson in attacking the United States Bank; that term was used by Davy Crockett in 1834 to say, "I might easily have been mistaken for one of the Kitchen Cabinet, I looked so much like a ghost." Since Jackson's time, however, the term has gained respectability in political talk.

The practice of filibustering, or using uninterrupted hours of talk to defeat a political measure, has been identified by various "talk" terms. TALK AGAINST TIME, for example, means to forestall a vote by continuous talking. *Democratic Review* in 1838 mentioned "a minority, however small, who may determine to 'talk against time.' " By the late nineteenth century, the preferred phrase was TO TALK TO DEATH, a way to prevent a bill's passage by discussing it until the time of adjournment, when no vote may be taken.

Animal terms have also gained respectability in politics. Political errors, for instance, have occasionally taken picturesque animal phrases for their depiction. Choosing the wrong person, for instance, was GETTING THE WRONG PIG BY THE TAIL. (A similar term was "getting the wrong sow by the ear.") John Bartlett quoted from an 1848 letter by a politician accused of switching party allegiance; the politician explained that "the Whigs supposed they could by some means make me a traitor to my party. But, sir, as the old saying is, they got the wrong pig by the tail." A later steamboat variant was WAKING UP THE WRONG PASSENGER, alluding to the disgruntlement of any passenger awakened unnecessarily at the wrong port.

BEEF TAX began in the eighteenth century not as a tax on cattle or on complaints. Instead, the phrase referred to a tax that could be paid in beef. This obsolete phrase was reported in Virginia in 1781: "Convinced of the impossibility of collecting the Beef Tax, in this County, I have agreed to accept of the People, the same quantity of Pork." More unusual was the BACHELOR'S TAX, specifically a tax upon unmarried men, explained in 1821 when in New York "A bill has been introduced into the legislature of this state, laying a tax upon bachelors over the age of 28 years, for the support of Female Literature." Mentioned in the eighteenth century, that tax was also mentioned in an Oklahoma newspaper in 1932: "Conner will propose a bachelor tax on all single men 30 years of age, increasing the tax progressively according to age."

The least worthy talk, however, takes the name of WEASEL WORDS. Teddy Roosevelt, who had also helped establish the Tennis Cabinet, popularized this alliterative phrase for the use of meaningless words. His source for the term may have been a *Century Magazine* article in 1900 by Stewart Chaplin, who explained the name: "Weasel words are words that suck all the life out of the words next to them, just as a weasel sucks an egg and leaves the shell. If you heft the egg afterward, it's as light as a feather, and not very filling when you're hungry; but a basketful of them would make quite a show, and would bamboozle the unwary."

Frustrated by such weak wording, Roosevelt offered this example: "You can have 'universal training,' or you can have 'voluntary training,' but when you use the word 'voluntary' to qualify the word 'universal,' you are using a weasel word; it has sucked all the meaning out of 'universal.' The words flatly contradict." By the middle of this century, the phrase had become a verb, and in 1948 the *Salt Lake Tribune* urged the best possible communication: "Let's not weasel-word. Let's say just what we mean."

CHAPTER 12

PREJUDICE

$\mathcal{N}$ot everybody appreciated the directness of Americans in the days leading up to World War II. An editorial writer for a Tokyo newspaper cogently summarized the Japanese view in 1939: "Americans generally are an arrogant, self-centered, dogmatic and unreflecting lot. What they call frankness is merely the result of prejudice."

The Latin motto on our national seal and our money, E PLURIBUS UNUM, means "Out of many, one." It was first used by the ancient Roman poet Virgil to describe the blending of many colors into one. Two thousand years after Virgil, America's writers and politicians still struggle to define that blending in appropriate terms.

"Here individuals of all nations are melted into a new race of men, whose labors and posterity will one day cause great changes in the world," wrote a Frenchman who lived in America in 1782.

America's metaphorical "melting pot," the forerunner phrase of today's "multiculturalism," applies perhaps more fittingly to the nation's language than to its populace. The metaphor may well have begun with that 1782 observation by J. Hector St. John, pseudonym of Michel Guillaume Jean de Crèvecoeur, the French essayist who wrote *Letters from an American Farmer.* His description of being "melted into a new race" was only part of his declaration of a Caucasian background: "What then is the American, this new man? He is either an European, or the descendant of an European, hence that strange mixture of blood, which you will find in no other country. I could point out to you a family whose grandfather was an Englishman, whose wife was Dutch, whose son married a French woman, and whose present four sons have now four wives of different nations."

Crèvecoeur's prophecy probably inspired the turn-of-the-century Jewish playwright Israel Zangwill to title his 1908 work *The Melting Pot.* In that play's first act comes the earliest appearance of the telling expression: "America is God's crucible, the great melting pot where all the races of Europe are melting and reforming."

During World War I, Woodrow Wilson spoke of an American crucible, "a great melting-pot in which we must compound a precious metal. That metal is the metal of nationality." Later in the century, another American president began to change the image. "We become not a melting pot," said Jimmy Carter in a 1976 speech in Pittsburgh, "but a beautiful mosaic. Different people, different beliefs, different yearnings, different hopes, different dreams." Even more recent is the multicultural image of the salad bowl, a gathering of diversity that allows for difference in commonality. The emphasis of each of these metaphors is upon treating those of other races with tolerance and dignity.

Opponents of racial harmony, however, popularized MIS-CEGENATION, which came into the language during the Civil War. Allegedly coined in 1863 by David Goodman Croly, a New York pamphleteer, this negative noun was formed by combining the Latin terms for "to mix" and "race." It became an attack term for any marriage between members of different races.

IN THE MINORITY

The battle against prejudice has proved itself to be a powerful motivator in the coining of new American vocabulary.

Among the effects of that multicultural awareness has been the advent of "political correctness." The initials "P.C." have long been current in the American language, used for "Peace Corps" and "postcard," as well as for "police chief" and "personal computer." Those two letters, however, are now employed almost exclusively as a shortening of "politically correct." That phrase, which had been in occasional use since the eighteenth century, first appeared in its "politically liberal or radical" sense in Toni Cade Bambara's 1970 anthology *The Black Woman:* "A man can be politically correct and a chauvinist too." In 1975, Karen De Crow, who was then president of NOW (the National Organization for Women), announced that the organization was headed in the "intellectually and politically correct direction." Today the phrase is primarily used as an attack term, particularly whenever conservatives want to attack what they consider the conformity of language and thinking by liberals, described since 1951 as KNEE-JERK for having automatic or predictable responses.

Language of racism and sexism, though, dates back to the beginnings of colonial America, and the history of such language reflects the changes in American society over the centuries. In the past generation, for example, "blacks" replaced "Negroes" as the preferred racial designation for those now known as "African-Americans." That term has been around since a Civil War song that referred in 1863 to "African-American citizens," but whether the label chosen as a self-description should be hyphenated remains a matter of controversy. Similarly, "Caucasian-American" has failed to catch on as a synonym for "white," although the more recent use of ANGLO, a parallel of LATINO for anyone of Hispanic background, seems to be spreading, at least among African-American speakers.

Past examples of hyphenation in the United States include "Italian-Americans" and "Irish-Americans." By the turn of the century, though, the phrase HYPHENATED AMERICAN was used as a slur to denounce immigrants for failing to assimilate fully. In 1915, Teddy Roosevelt spoke before the Knights of Columbus in New York and announced, "There is no room in this country for hyphenated Americanism." Roosevelt's warning continued: "The one absolutely certain way of bringing this nation to ruin, of preventing all possibility of its continuing to be a nation at all, would be to permit it to become a tangle of squabbling nationalities."

World War I inflamed the anti-immigration sentiment, and the former president denounced hyphenation in even stronger terms of patriotism in 1918: "There can be no fifty-fifty Americanism in this country. There is room here only for one hundred percent Americanism." In the next decade, the *New York Observer* applied the term HUNDRED-PERCENTISM to patriotism that becomes exaggerated, and that paper published an opinion in 1928 that "New York is not the place for the Hundred-Percenters. I certainly never met any." By 1930, however, the playwright George Bernard Shaw undermined Roosevelt's percentages with the comment, "I have defined the hundred per cent American as ninety-nine percent an idiot."

As each wave of immigration has entered the country, terms of intolerance and bigotry have appeared. During the Irish influx of the 1840s, for example, the average Irishman became stereotyped with the name of Patrick. As the Irish labored to help build America's railways, their own songs emphasized the anti-Irish sentiment and stereotypical treatment.

"In eighteen-hundred-and-forty-two," one song began, "I left the old world for the new . . . to work upon the railway." A later stanza of that song lamented the dishonesty of the American bosses, particularly those of British ancestry, who managed the Irish workers:

> The boss's name, it was Tom King.
> He kept a store to rob the men,
> A Yankee clerk with ink and pen
> To cheat Pat on the railway.

That sense of Yankee trickery is as old as the country, but the slurs that have resulted are mostly gentle jesting (as in "Yankee cunning") compared with the harsher racial insults that suffuse American history.

Unworthy of reviving are those many racial slurs that have crowded the American language. Long before the old expression PEOPLE OF COLOR became prominent as a multicultural label three decades ago, there were the pointed abbreviations "F. M. C." and "F. W. C." Dating from before the Civil War, those initials were applied as early as 1840 to "Free Man of Color" and "Free Woman of Color." A 1936 history, however, noted the limited numbers in Louisiana before the War Between the States: "These free men and women of color—after the American occupation they were commonly designated in the newspapers and in many legal documents, simply by the initials 'f.m.c.' and 'f.w.c.'—never formed more than a small proportion of the population."

Just as African-Americans have suffered from the abuses of prejudice, Native Americans have also been derogated since colonial days. A put-down such as INDIAN GIVER for one who takes back a present, or HONEST INDIAN for one who is rarely truthful, has its origins in racial prejudice. Today's alliterative term "designated driver," indicating a partygoer who drinks no alcohol and drives the drinkers home afterward, comes from an older idea expressed with a racist term, DO (or PLAY) THE SOBER INDIAN. An 1832 work on social events described this practice: "During these drinking fits, there is always one at least of the party who remains sober, in order to secure the knives, &c. Hence the Americans derive the cant phrase of 'doing the sober Indian' which they apply to any one of a company who will not drink fairly."

Anti-Indian feelings were evident throughout much of colonial American writing and in the literature of the new nation. When James Fenimore Cooper wrote about using angles to determine the location of beehives, he added a note in 1848 that "Indians are not expert . . . on account of the 'angle-ing' part of the process, which much exceeds their skill in mathematics." A band of the Blackfoot tribe received the American name of "Bloods," perhaps from their practice of painting their faces with red streaks from ear to ear; by 1858, "Blood Tubs" was the name of a gang of Baltimore youths, and although that term is now obsolete, BLOODS is still used by other American gangs.

For more than a century, INDIAN has been used in America as a synonym for "temper." An 1889 slang dictionary offered a series of such terms: "Irish, Indian, Dutch (American), all of these words are used to signify anger or arousing temper." Of those prejudices, however, the attack on Native Americans was the severest. That slang dictionary also observed, "But to say that one has his 'Indian up,' implies a great degree of vindictiveness, while Dutch wrath is stubborn but yielding to reason."

SEX CHANGE

Throughout its history the American language has shown itself capable of sexism as well as of racism in its prejudice.

Almost a century before women received the right to vote,

a common term for a female citizen was AMERICANESS. Now obsolete, that 1830s noun was found in an 1879 report in a San Francisco newspaper: "One of these rascally responses threw the young Americaness into such fury that she was taken with a fit of hysterics." MAYORESS and LIBRARIANESS were also tested, but perhaps the most unwieldy title proved to be "SUPERINTENDENTESS of Education"; even before the vote, women voters received the title of VOTRESSES.

Other examples of sexism in the language were rampant a century ago. LITTLE WOMAN was in use by 1881 as a term for a man's spouse; seventy years later, Mitford Mathews continued to defend the phrase as being "an affectionate or appreciative designation for a wife." Deservedly obsolete is MAIDENLAND, a Virginia form of dowry. In 1859, Bartlett defined this marriage arrangement as "land that a man gets with his wife, and which he loses at her death."

Also gone from the language is a Civil War variant of the still-current WAITRESS. An 1861 diary placed quotation marks around a synonym for that server: WAITER GIRL. "The conduct of the 'waiter girls' with the frequenters of the place," the diarist huffed, "is simply shocking." From that term came the longer and more sexist phrase of PRETTY WAITER GIRL, a Missouri use in 1875 for a "beer-slinger," and still used after the turn of the century in place of the 1834 noun "waitress." Today's nonsexist variation is the robotlike noun WAITRON, a recent coinage meant deliberately to conceal the sex of the SERVER, a less-contrived usage to achieve the same effect.

WAR WOMAN, on the other hand, was used in various ways as a complimentary expression. The earliest use of that term served to depict a priestess or female sage among Native Americans. A 1765 memoir commented that "Old warrior likewise, or war-women, . . . have the title of Beloved." Two decades later, another writer offered a more detailed glimpse of this female figure: "In every Indian village, the war-woman also is a kind of oracle; by dreams and presages, she directs the hunters to their prey, and the warriors to the enemy." After the Revolutionary War, the phrase was also applied to a resident of Georgia named Nancy Hart, whose strategies and courage in fighting the British earned her the admiring title of war woman.

A woman devoted to farming was known in the late nineteenth century as a FARMERINE. A New York newspaper editorialized in 1888, "Then the average farmerine will be as near the millennium as she is ever likely to get." By the time of World War I, the preferred synonym was FARMERETTE, but that term is now as obsolete as the name for the overalls she wore: *The New Republic* noted in 1917 that "The newspapers were photographing farmerettes, and the department stores advertised a strange garment called WOMANALLS."

GIVING OFFENSE

Other prejudicial terms have been slower to depart the American vocabulary.

The racist CHINAMAN'S CHANCE, for instance, is a colloquialism intended to express an extreme unlikelihood of success. A generation ago, the American lexicographer Mitford Mathews speculated on the uncertain history of this phrase, which may date back to the western gold rush of 1849: "This expression originated in California, possibly in the days of the 'Forty-niners.' It may have stemmed from the practice by Chinese miners of working over tailings [mining scraps or leftovers] left by white miners where their chances of gain were regarded as meager. . . . Or it may have grown out of the early intense hostility against Chinese that developed in that region." The opposite of "Chinaman's chance" is the 1845 phrase WHITE MAN'S CHANCE, to denote a good or likely chance of succeeding.

Neither have culturally sensitive names become universal

in the United States. A Florida carryout, for example, uses mock pidgin English in its name, the "Chinee Takee Outee." At the same time, an Arizona hotel's restaurant features a "Co-Cheese burger," based on the name of the Apache leader Cochise.

SQUAW, although its usage has been widely criticized by Native Americans, may still be heard. This term is from an Algonquian word for "woman," although some American Indians claim that the exact meaning is "vagina." In his dictionary of Americanisms, Mathews defined SQUAW MAN as "a white man married to an Indian woman, or an Indian who does woman's work." An 1877 explanation of that term portrayed such a man in western dialect as "One that ain't allowed ter fight, or hunt, or git married, or own hosses; but has tew stay about the camp with the squaws all the time." By contrast, the Abenaki term for a man is SANNUP, specifically an ordinary warrior, separated in class structure by that native tribe from a chief, called a SAGAMORE by the Abenaki; in a 1628 Massachusetts historical record, this class separation was made clear: "Sanops must speak to sanops, and sagamores to sagamores."

Although current in the name of Washington's professional football team, REDSKIN often carries the notation of "offensive" in modern dictionaries. The term, now widely considered a slur in reference to aboriginal Americans, appeared in a 1699 history of colonial days and demonstrated the animosity between the natives and the colonists, who reported, "Ye firste Meetinge House was solid mayde to withstande ye wicked onsaults of ye Red Skins." That distrust also led to the phrase RED DEVILS, found in an 1834 comment about the strained relations with Indians in Kentucky: "If a man should stand addlin his brains about the right and wrong of the thing, the red devils would just knock them out to settle the matter."

Attempts to assimilate natives to colonial ways led to such expressions as RED BRETHREN and RED CHILDREN in the early 1800s. The racial designation of RED was repeated in the nineteenth century by Tatanka Yotanka, also known as Sitting Bull. According to Justin Kaplan's edition of *Bartlett's Quotations,* it appeared in a statement by Sitting Bull when the Indian leader asked pointed questions that began, "What treaty that the white man ever made with us have they kept? . . . Is it wrong for me to love my own? Is it wicked for me because my skin is red? Because I am a Sioux; because I was born where my father lived; because I would die for my people and my country?"

As many Americans have grown more sensitive to their choice of words, once-familiar expressions no longer seem clear. FITIFIED, for example, was an 1822 southernism still in use more than a century later. The adjective, however, means "epileptic," and the medical term is the preferred word these days.

On the other hand, MORON remains in use as an insult. That noun was once applied to any adult diagnosed as having the mental faculties of a child between the ages of eight and twelve; homes for those known as "feeble-minded" took on the term MORON COLONIES in the 1920s. In that same decade, "moron" was also defined as a sexual pervert, with *American Mercury* commenting in 1924, "So long as morons are permitted to remain at large there will be crime waves." Today's use of the noun is less specific and applies to any foolish or stupid person. "I'm surrounded by morons," announced the central character in the 1980s television comedy *Mama's Family.*

Dictionaries of recent vintage have grown more careful in their definitions. Noah Webster's original 1806 edition of his dictionary offered the neutral definition of STATESMAN as "a man employed in public affairs"; the same dictionary, however, defined STATESWOMAN as "a woman who meddles in public matters." Sexism has continued in American definitions into the current century. Less than fifty years ago, an

American dictionary defined the political "House page" as "a boy serving as a page in the House of Representatives," a position now available to females as well.

CULTURE SHOCK

As reactions against prejudice, terms that suggest cultural sensitivity are being tried out in the vocabulary of modern Americans. A chart in a 1996 issue of *American Speech,* for instance, offered examples of cultural insensitivity as well as the politically correct variations. Here are half a dozen of the terms:

NOT P.C.	P.C.
girl, lady	woman, womyn
sex	gender
blind	visually impaired
handicapped	challenged
Oriental	Asian
salesman	sales person, sales clerk

Perhaps the best indication of the language's ability to change is in the etymology of the noun "girl"; in the fourteenth century, that word was originally applied to a child of either sex— or gender.

As the language grows to assimilate and accommodate, examples of awareness about racism and sexism may be found throughout society. Visitors to Williamsburg, Virginia, may now take "Other Half" tours to see the colonial living conditions of African-Americans, and in 1997 a Japanese internment camp from World War II was opened to tourists in California. Viewers of *Star Trek* and its subsequent series

have witnessed a significant linguistic change; the original series described a mission "to boldly go where no man has gone
before," but its sequels changed "man" to the nonsexist
"one."

Similarly, in the latest revision of *The United Methodist
Hymnal,* a religious lyric contains a reference to GITCHI MAN-
ITOU, a Native American term that is equated with "Great
God." That book of church songs also includes several trans-
lations of a familiar hymn. Here are the opening lines as they
were phonetically transcribed from singing at the Oklahoma
Indian Missionary Conference and printed in the 1989 hym-
nal:

OOH NAY THLA NAH, HEE OO WAY GEE
(Cherokee)

SHILOMBISH HOLITOPA MA!
(Choctaw)

PO YA FEK CHA HE THLAT AT TET
(Creek)

DAW KEE DA HA DAWTSAHY HE
TSOW'HAW
(Kiowa)

Each of those transcriptions represents the start of John Newton's 1779 hymn, which in English begins, "Amazing grace!
How sweet the sound . . ." Newton had himself been the captain of a slave-trading ship who renounced the evils of his past
and devoted himself to a strict religious life in his native England.

Native Americanisms

CARIBOU Micmac for "large antlered deer" or "reindeer"

HALO Chinook Jargon for "none" or "not at all"

HOGAN Navajo for "house of logs and mud"

KACHINA Tewa for "dancing spirit" (often represented as a doll)

NETOP Narraganset for "companion" or "friend"

SAGAMORE Abenaki for "title of leader or chief"

TEMESCAL Nahuatl for "steam bath" or "place of steam"

TEPEE Siouan for "lodge" or "dwelling place"

TOBOGGAN Algonquian for "fast or flat-bottomed sled"

TOTEM Ojibwa for "customary symbol or representation"

Native words abound in American English, but a number of cautions must be offered with their translations. For instance, Mitford M. Mathews explained the complicated history of "Tennessee" in his *Dictionary of Americanisms*. That proper noun, he wrote, is the result of a double mispronunciation: "From American Indian but otherwise obscure. Probably a mispronunciation of a Cherokee mispronunciation of a Creek name."

Also, a native term may be subject to the bias of the English-speaking interpreter. The term for an important person, HIGH-MUCK-A-MUCK, has been traced in the Chinook Jargon to a combination of two terms, neither one being "high." The first is *hiu,* meaning "much," and the second is *muckamuck* for "food or drink." This image, still in popular use, has nothing to do with a high position, but rather denotes somebody who is considered important because of having extensive provisions.

Many Americanized words from natives are based on the understanding of the nonnative listener. In an 1898 history of the Indians, a writer gives a ceremonial pole the name FABUSSA, its spelling based on his understanding of the word's pronunciation. He also explained what he understood of the pole's mystical significance: "The evening before their departure a fabussa (pole, pronounced as Fa-bus-sah) was firmly set up in the ground at the centre point of their encampment, by direction of their chief medicine man . . . to whom . . . the Great Spirit had revealed that the Fabussa would indicate on the following morning, the direction they should march by its leaning." The reason for the name, however, remains unknown.

Also uncertain is the name of the Indian known as SQUANTO. It appears in dictionaries of Americanisms under the alternative spelling "Squantum," but there is controversy about its origin. In Frederick Hodge's Indian history, A. F. Chamberlain is quoted as saying, "The place name Squantum is said to be derived from Tisquantum, or Tasquantum, the appellation of a Massachusetts Indian, generally known to the settlers about Plymouth as Squantum or Squanto. . . . In all probability the word goes back to this personal name in the Massachuset dialect of Algonquian, signifying 'door,' 'entrance.' " A more recent explanation in the journal *American Folk-Lore* contradicts this theory: "The name explains itself by the verb *musquantum* (he is angry) and by Roger Williams's remark, 'They [the Narraganset Indians] will say, when an ordinary accident, as a fall, has occurred to somebody: *musquantam manit* (God was angry and did it).' "

Cultural differences have also led to misunderstandings about native terms in Hawaii. In *Da Kine Talk,* the linguist Elizabeth Ball Carr pointed out that the word HULA was defined in the unabridged second edition of *Webster's New International Dictionary* as "A native Hawaiian woman's dance. It is of a mimetic and often lascivious character, and is usually accompanied with rhythmic drumming and chanting."

According to Carr, "This grossly incorrect definition of HULA exasperated some residents of Hawaii, where parents from all ethnic groups encourage their daughters to learn the hula in the hope that they may acquire the grace of motion of the dance and an understanding of the poetic interpretation." The linguist specializing in the fiftieth state was encouraged by the change of definition that appeared in the third edition of *Webster's Unabridged*: "A sinuous mimetic Polynesian dance of conventional form and topical adaptation performed by men and women singly or together and usually accompanied by chants and rhythmic drumming."

AGE-WISE

The prejudice identified in 1969 as AGISM (or AGEISM) has endured, with many American terms still sounding critical of aging and the elderly.

When Thurgood Marshall retired from the Supreme Court in 1992, he answered a reporter's question about age: "What's wrong with me? I'm old. I'm getting old and coming apart." Awareness about the aging of the general population has led to such terms as "ageism," used in charges of discrimination against the elderly, and "chronologically enhanced," a humorous addition to many P.C. phrases attempting to avoid such limiting words as "impaired" or "challenged."

As the population ages, the language will add more words, some of them perhaps reflecting the insensitivity of existing terms. During the Civil War, GRANNIFIED came into use as an adjective meaning "like an elderly woman or granny"; its use in a Connecticut newspaper was even more insensitive in describing "that querulous and grannified manner peculiar to old people who have outlived their usefulness." In the 1990s, the lexicographer Anne H. Soukhanov reported the rise of the phrase GRANNY DUMPING, which she defined in her book *Word Watch* as offensive slang for "abandonment of an elderly person by relatives, a landlord, or a caregiver, typically by leaving the person along with a suitcase of essential personal effects in a hospital emergency room." Synonyms for the surly phrase include such terms as ELDERLY ABANDONMENT and PACKED-SUITCASE SYNDROME.

The United States itself has been subjected to a reverse ageism, a sense of newness that was first recognized in print by Mark Twain in his book *Life on the Mississippi,* published in 1883. "The world and the books," Twain noted, "are so accustomed to use, and over-use, the word 'new' in connection with our country, that we early get and permanently retain the impression that there is nothing old about it." More than two centuries after the nation's formation, America has added an extensive vocabulary of "old" terms, particularly in its names and nicknames. Sometimes the phrases have been put-downs, including OLD CORNSTALK for an elderly man thought to be ineffectual, OLD GIRL used by a husband to refer to his wife, and even OLD DRIVER, an 1877 euphemism for the devil.

Other "old" terms, however, retain respect and dignity, but the language has a distance to go for historical cleansing. In 1998, according to the Associated Press, Virginia prepared to replace the historical markers along the state's roadways. To be deleted were all references to American Indians as "heathens," "savages," and "half-breeds."

CHAPTER 13

PASSION

*D*espite being the father of an entire country, George Washington is not normally pictured as a passionate man. His portrait artist, however, disagreed. "All his features," said Gilbert Stuart after completing a painting of Washington in 1795, "were indicative of the most ungovernable passions, and had he been born in the forests . . . he would have been the fiercest man among the savage tribes."

Even the harmless drudges who concoct dictionaries have their passionate moments. "I finished writing my dictionary," Noah Webster once wrote about his foremost accomplishment, "in January 1825 at my lodging. . . . When I had come to the last word, I was seized with a trembling, which made it somewhat difficult to hold my pen steady for writing. The cause seems to have been the thought that I might not then live to finish the work, or the thought that I was so near the end of my labors. But I summoned strength to finish the last word, and then walking about the room, a few minutes, I recovered." The first edition of his *American Dictionary of the English Language* was published three years later.

Oddly enough, when Noah Webster completed the first major American dictionary, the lexicographer was nowhere near the United States. Instead, he finished his language labor of love during a visit to Cambridge, England. The finished product included both the unavoidable (the verb AMERICAN-IZE) and the unwieldy (the rare verb CITIZENIZE, meaning "to make a citizen").

Edgar Allan Poe, a contemporary of Webster, was equally passionate about the American language. The coiner of TIN-TINNABULATION in 1831 for the musical sound of ringing bells, the poet Poe opined optimistically that "I do not believe that any thought, properly so called, is out of the reach of language. I have never had a thought which I could not set down in words." (Despite such optimism about the American tongue, however, his stories make contradictory statements about "unutterable horror and awe, for which the language of mortality has no sufficiently energetic expression" and about French phrases for which, Poe says, "there is no exact English equivalent.")

The passions of American citizens have long helped shape the language, particularly in the century and a half since Webster's death. Words and phrases new to the American tongue reflect our enduring national obsessions. Sex and violence, sports and cars, food and fads—all have contributed coinages to the American cant.

LOVE HANDLES

From "beliked" to "kiss-me-quick," the American language has embraced more than its share of romantic and sexual terms.

The Old World practice of BUNDLING carried over to the New World with a passionate enthusiasm. This courtship custom, based on the verb BUNDLE meaning "to wrap or dress warmly," was first mentioned in English in 1781. During a night of bundling, an unmarried couple could share a bed without undressing; this chaste coupling allowed a romantic relationship to develop while maintaining propriety before family members. The main current use, of computers shipped with software packages, is disappointing by comparison.

From the early days of the country came BELIKED, an Americanized version of the fourteenth-century "beloved." A western writer observed that "I do believe me and Nancy was beliked by the Indians, and many's the venison and turkey they fotch'd us as a sort of present." Similarly homespun was the KISS-ME-QUICK, a quilted bonnet that would have been, according to John Bartlett, "chiefly used to cover the head by ladies when going to parties, or the theatre."

In fact, romantic-sounding terms have suffused the Americanisms of the last two centuries. LOST MOON, for example, appeared in the eighteenth century among terms from native calendars. In 1778, a traveler among the Indians noted, "Some nations among them reckon their years by moons, and make them consist of twelve synodical or lunar months, observing, when thirty moons have waned, to add a supernumerary one, which they term the lost moon; and then begin to count as before."

The naming of America's flowers often borrowed romantic phrases, including LOVE'S TEST, also known as the *common everlasting* and used in predicting romances. Less romantic is the plant phrase TO GO WHERE THE WOODBINE TWINETH, meaning "to fail or come to nothing." When people or money mysteriously disappeared in the late nineteenth century, that phrase was employed. In 1897, *The Congressional Record* referred to a defeated bill as one that "goes 'where the woodbine twineth,' " and the phrase continued to be used until after the First World War.

· · ·

By the time of the Second World War, America's slang terms for feelings of love contained several feverish phrases. Here are a dozen:

arm-in-arm it
feel you have a feeling you never felt before
go for in the I Care manner
goona-goona
heart stroke
just one of those things
mooey-mooey
romantricks
roses and raptures
tenth word in a telegram
uh-huh
woo-poo

The shine of wartime lovers was known as GLOWMANCE (from a blend of "glowing" and "romance"). A fourth member added to the ETERNAL TRIANGLE could create a WRECK-TANGLE. Stealing somebody else's date was MALE ROBBERY, while romance at night was known as DARKSETTING.

Today's language of love leans toward the raunchy rather than the romantic, more frequently featuring the public display than the personal. (LOVE HANDLES, a late-sixties term for rolls of fat on the side of the body, is one of the few nonexplicit LOVE terms of recent years.) The 1965 TALK SHOW led to the 1980s phenomenon of TALK RADIO (sometimes described as ALL-TALK, often taking place during DRIVE TIME) and, in the 1990s, to the specialization of SEX TALK, often discussed by a SHOCK JOCK. Technological advances have also been reflected in the current decade's obsessions with PHONE SEX as well as the laptop lust known as CYBERSEX, jocularly known as TELEDILDONICS.

Perhaps the ultimate statement of America's passion for passion appears as an epitaph for the poet Robert Frost. On his grave in Bennington, Vermont, is a line from his 1942 poem "The Lesson for Today." Its singular sentiment, marking Frost's resting place, is the observation that "I had a lover's quarrel with the world."

HAVE GUN, WILL TRAVEL

"America's highways are becoming a war zone," the actor Robert Stack intoned on the 1990s television series *Unsolved Mysteries,* leading into a report on ROAD RAGE. The improvement of transportation across the country has led to an increase in violence and the language of lawlessness.

As pathways across the country became more established, ROAD phrases began to enlarge the American language. ROAD AGENT began as a westernism during the Civil War as the term for a highway robber. In 1863, a traveler in the Rocky Mountains observed a nervous man and his purse, which "he had thrown away in the grass, taking us for road agents." From that phrase came a longer term for the thief's activity in a 1947 history: "When Vigilantes took over law enforcement, highway robbery was apt to increase, for they simply drove the crooks out of town and some took to road agentry."

Such a highwayman also came to be known for the ROAD AGENT SPIN, which was a way to spin a revolver backward instead of forward on the trigger finger. In New England, however, the western label developed a far different sense. After World War II, the phrase became a synonym for "roadmaster or surveyor," used in a 1945 commentary on "political discussions, all the way from who will be the next road agent to who will be the next president."

Since the turn of the century, ROAD COMPANY has been theatrical parlance for a touring company, and in 1904 ROAD

GANG was the term for any group of prisoners sentenced to work on roads. Much more recent is the complimentary SMART ROAD, meaning high-tech highways capable of monitoring traffic and travel problems. Less successful has been the development of AUTOIST, a 1903 alternative to "motorist"; an issue of *Scientific American* referred in 1903 to "bills giving equal rights to autoists and the drivers of horses."

The vocabulary of violence, however, continued to grow in the 1980s with DRIVE-BY to describe random or casual shooting, as by members of a street gang, later extended to refer to any quick casual or random act, as in "drive-by delivery." (Those who leave gas stations without paying are DRIVE-OFFs.) ROAD RAGE, a late-1980s term that rose to prominence in the mid-1990s, is the alliterative phrase for the fury that develops out of driver frustration.

GOOD SPORTS

The language has also continued to flourish with the terms of partying and playing. Many metaphors from sports and games have added coloring to the American lexicon, with baseball alone adding such familiar expressions as WAY OFF BASE and OUT IN LEFT FIELD, the semantic explanation for which is still a subject of debate.

ANYBODY'S GAME is a twentieth-century variant of the earlier ANYBODY'S RACE, a metaphor for any contest too close to call. In Elkins, West Virginia, *The Randolph Enterprise* commented in 1930, "This will probably be a close game and anybody's game to the finish." According to the *Ball Players' Chronology* of 1867, PLAY BALL! was already in use soon after the Civil War for the umpire's cry to begin a baseball game, although major league rules require the umpire to say only "Play!" By the 1890s, the phrase was extended to mean "get going"; ten years after that, TO PLAY BALL WITH became a slang phrase for "to cooperate with or go along with." A 1930 work on underworld graft in New York stated, "The police of Buffalo are too dumb—it would be redundant, I suppose, to say 'and honest'—to play ball with the hold-up mobs." BALLPLAYER became an underworld term for a person willing to engage in graft; it dates to the 1940s. The location of a baseball game, 1899's BALLPARK, was pressed into service in the 1950s in the sense "an approximate range"—usually in the phrase "in the ballpark," and by the 1960s we saw the transformation into the adjectival ballpark, as in "a ballpark figure."

Simple victory, in metaphorical terms, was not enough. Instead, the devil himself had to be vanquished. Since the country's formation, Southerners have referred to roundabout methods of victory as WHIPPING THE DEVIL AROUND A STUMP. Another phrase about the devil refers to a more decisive form of winning: BEAT THE DEVIL AND CARRY A RAIL. In 1872, a newspaper in Little Rock, Arkansas, editorialized that "For a sample of honesty this beats the devil and carries a rail." Why the rail? This phrase is derived from a rural practice in unevenly matched contests; the superior contestant, particularly in running a foot race, would be handed a rail to carry as a handicap.

HARDBALL is the primary baseball metaphor of politics. Used for more than a century as a synonym for "baseball," PLAYING HARDBALL has taken on a nastier sense of using rough tactics to gain an advantage. The 1926 SOFTBALL, in contrast, has gained a metaphorical meaning in journalism of a deliberately easy or vague question posed to a candidate.

GAME PLAN has been used since the 1960s for a political strategy, and the basketball defense of FULL-COURT PRESS for an extreme effort came into politics a decade later. A LEVEL PLAYING FIELD is meant to provide an equal opportunity for everyone involved, in sports or in the even more competitive world of business.

The term FOOTBALL dates back to the fifteenth century, and it remains a most powerful force in political punditry. PO-LITICAL FOOTBALL refers to any issue or object that becomes unfairly turned into a controversy by politicians. (In his *New Political Dictionary,* William Safire notes the more recent "ominous" use of "football" for the metal briefcase used to carry the secret codes needed by the president to begin a nuclear attack.)

Perhaps the prevalent football metaphor is that of the quarterback. Instead of the verb "to lead," a person in charge will QUARTERBACK an effort. Critics of the effort are known as MONDAY-MORNING QUARTERBACKS, in reference to the next-day follow-up for games played on Sundays. Finally, a quarterback making an all-out effort at the end of a game might throw a HAIL MARY PASS, a long pass with little chance of success. Figurative use of this phrase was popularized during the Gulf War by Gen. H. Norman Schwarzkopf, who compared a flanking maneuver to the play during a press briefing.

The power of sports terms in politics has been evident at least since this simile by John F. Kennedy: "Politics is like football. If you see daylight, go through the hole."

PLAYING THE ODDS

A passion for competition has long pervaded the American psyche. Struggling to win titles and trophies has reached more often to the ridiculous than to the sublime.

In Virginia, the annual Highland County Maple Festival in March features competing methods of SUGAR-MAKING, the making of maple syrup. This process of reducing maple-tree sap into syrup originated with American Indians, who referred to it as *seensibankwut.* The Treasure Mountain Festival, held each September in Pendleton County, West Virginia, includes a variety of contests referred to as CALLINGS. These competitions require contestants to reproduce the sounds of various birds native to the local forests. "Turkey calling" and "owl hooting" are among the types of talents represented there, and a Georgia fund-raising celebration culminates in a KISS-A-PIG campaign.

Indiana, however, offers what is perhaps the strangest competition to contribute to the American language. Purdue University sponsors the annual BUG BOWL, its name based on oversized sports events like the Super Bowl and the various college bowl games. Among the creative contests in this gathering is CRICKET SPITTING, a championship that rewards the expectoration of dead bugs for distance. (According to the Associated Press, signs marking the chocolate-covered-cricket stand at the Bug Bowl promised "tastes like chicken" and "50 million lizards can't be wrong.")

Winning phrases of nineteenth-century America include TO TAKE THE SHINE OFF, meaning "to excel or surpass," and TO WALK INTO, "to get the upper hand or take advantage." The apparent winner of any contest would be well advised not TO WHISTLE BEFORE YOU ARE OUT OF THE WOODS. That expression, which appeared in a New York newspaper more than a century ago, means "to exult or celebrate before you are out of danger."

MINTY FRESH

America's excessive fascination with fads, from fashion to food, has recently provided the country with a most appropriate coinage: FADDICTION.

The passion for new words has often led to faddish phrases, terms that were probably never intended to last long in the language. Dictionaries of expressions from the Old West, for instance, point to the many and varied terms used for the long-favored cattle known as the Texas longhorn. With its wide span of horns, it has taken on such disparate nicknames as SEA LION and HORNED JACK RABBIT; other references to this wild cow of Texas have included CACTUS BOOMER and COASTER, TWISTHORN and MOSSYBACK. Similarly, the western restaurant took on a variety of names, from BEANERY and GREASE JOINT to FEEDBAG and GRUB HOUSE and even SWALLOW-AND-GET-OUT TROUGH.

Terms that may or may not prove to be short-term ones are still coming into the language. The brevity of fads, for instance, has led to the coining of the trendy TRENDLET. In the field of health care, SUNDOWNING depicts a condition of Alzheimer's patients who tend to become more active at night.

The trend of SURFING as a technological term led from CHANNEL SURFING as a 1990 phrase for the quick clicking of a remote control from one television channel to another, to NET SURFING as a term for navigating the Internet, to SHOULDER SURFING for the criminal activity of trying to steal somebody else's telephone access code by looking over the shoulder of a person dialing a public phone. ELEVATOR SURFING is the "sport" of jumping on top of the outside of an elevator car while it is moving.

Surfing, though, is most closely associated with that huge source of recent vocabulary—the Internet. While some NET terms are older ones, pressed back into service, such as NEWBIE for a newcomer (from the Vietnam War) and LURKER for a person who watches but doesn't participate (from CB radio talk), most are brand-new coinages. EMOTICONS, or SMILEYS, are text characters joined to form symbols expressing feelings, such as :-), a sideways smiley face, for happiness. SNAIL MAIL is the horribly inefficient physical delivery of mail, as opposed to the faster E-MAIL, or electronic mail, now used to refer to an individual letter ("an E-mail") and as a verb meaning to send it. *E-* is one of the all-around winners of the modern computer age as a free-forming prefix.

E- has to compete with the even more common CYBER-,

originally found in the 1940s CYBERNETICS, a coinage of Norbert Wiener. The prefix got its biggest boost when novelist William Gibson used it in CYBERSPACE, now the catchall term for the wired world. Now we have CYBERCASH, CYBERCHAT, and even CYBERJEWELRY. The graphical WORLD WIDE WEB has been the inspiration for most of the surfing metaphors; to see it you need a BROWSER and to stay awake while waiting for HOME PAGES to scroll in, you need java, not to be confused with JAVA, a popular programming language.

You don't want to nibble on COOKIES, though these little electronic files are placed on your hard drive so that marketers can track your cyber-whereabouts. And the food you most definitely want to avoid is SPAM, the usual term for what is technically called Unsolicited Commercial E-mail (UCE). Spam got its name from a classic Monty Python routine where a chorus of Vikings shout "Spam, Spam, Spam, Spam," until they drown out everything else.

Based on the 1950s noun "brainstorming" is the more recent concept of BLAMESTORMING, a session for discussing a failed project and the person most worthy of being held responsible. The nineteenth-century BARNSTORMING, on the other hand, came from the practice of touring theatrical groups appearing in barns instead of theaters, and that term was picked up in this century for an electioneering style favored by politicians who make many short stops in their campaigns.

The process of word inflation has elevated the status of simpler terms like "fired" and "wordy." Since 1871, FIRE OUT has been used for "to toss a person from a place," shortened in the following decade to FIRE; the new term for that loss of position is the verb UNINSTALL, as well as larger-scale euphemisms such as DOWNSIZE, RIGHTSIZE, and MAKE REDUNDANT. Meanwhile, songs that were at one time called "wordy" are now known as LYRIC-INTENSIVE.

The entertainment world has been playing up other colorful coinages. The trend toward violence in horror pictures, once known as SLASHERS for the bloodletting of victims, has led to the use of SCREAMERS for films meant to elicit a sharp vocal response by shocked viewers. Striking a television set or other electronic device to improve its performance has taken on the jocular title of PERCUSSIVE MAINTENANCE. Television's readers of weather forecasts, now generally elevated to METEOROLOGISTS, have promoted SUCKER LULL, on the analogy of the sneaky "sucker punch," for the unsettling quiet before a hurricane hits.

At the cutting edge of the American language have been phrases pointing to various types of FRONTIER. In the early 1960s, John F. Kennedy's administration promoted the NEW FRONTIER, a phrase that was not very new. In 1934, *New Frontiers* was the title of a book by Henry A. Wallace, who became Franklin Delano Roosevelt's running mate in the 1940 presidential election. FINAL FRONTIER or LAST FRONTIER has also seen widespread use, applied sometimes to oceanic exploration, sometimes to outer space, most prominently in the voice-over to the original *Star Trek* series.

Throughout the twentieth century, mobile Americans have also applied a wide range of names to their automobiles, particularly the JUNKERS or older models that provide recollections of the early days of automotive travel. Nicknames for aging or broken-down cars abound in the language, some more familiar than others.

Perhaps the best of the worst car terms is the EDSEL, named for Henry Ford's grandson. The ill-fated car given that name was first sold by the Ford Motor Company in 1957, and proved so unpopular that it was withdrawn from the market by 1959, and "Edsel" wheeled its way into the general language as a synonym for "failure." In a 1996 book, for instance, Judge Judith Sheindlin, known to television audiences as "Judge Judy," vividly depicted the state of America's family courts: "We taxpayers are paying for a Rolls-Royce juvenile system and we're getting an Edsel."

Sour Lemons

RATTLETRAP predating the automobile, an 1822 term applied a century later to any old car, particularly a noisy vehicle

JUNKHEAP a turn-of-the-century term, the only "old car" expression with roots dating back to Old English, in which "heap" meant "pile" or "large amount"

BUZZ-WAGON dting back to 1903, an old term for an old car

FLIVVER of unknown origin, a 1910 term for a cheap or small car

TIN LIZZIE a 1915 term for an old, inexpensive car, based on the nickname for the Model T

JALOPY of uncertain origin, a 1920s term for any dilapidated vehicle (the novelist John Steinbeck chose to spell it "gillopy")

MODEL T from an early Ford having two speeds, a term used since the 1940s for an outdated model

CLUNKER used since World War II for a worn-out vehicle

GRAVEYARD ON WHEELS a particularly graphic phrase from the 1950s for a dangerously old automobile

BOMB a 1969 term used in New York for a dilapidated car, preceded by Australian usage of the slang word in 1950 (A-BOMB was part of the slang of hot-rodders in the early 1950s, though for them it meant a souped-up Model A Ford)

CHAPTER 14

RESTLESSNESS

"There's no there there," commented a skeptical Gertrude Stein once in trying to define the city of Oakland, California. In her 1936 book, *The Geographical History of America,* Stein expanded her exploration in an attempt to define the entire nation. According to Stein, "In the United States, there is more room where nobody is than where anybody is. This is what makes America what it is."

Even more poetic is the explanation of our national character offered in 1943 by the poet Stephen Vincent Benét. "Americans," he wrote, "are always moving on."

Restlessness and travel have always been significant to the extension of the American language. From the aboriginal tribes who traversed the countryside before the United States became a country to the astronauts who have pushed the envelope to the moon and beyond, mobility marks the American way. Within such a mobile society, the terms that have developed often reflect a need or longing for travel.

Perhaps the most famous name in American literature, in fact, was a pseudonym drawn from the jargon of steamboat travel. Samuel Langhorne Clemens chose to publish his humor under the designation of "Mark Twain." The writer was quoted in a biography as explaining his decision: "I want to sign my articles . . . 'Mark Twain.' It is an old river term, a leadsman's call, signifying two fathoms—twelve feet."

That version of the story from 1863, the year his byline first appeared, seems more plausible than an alternative story from Nevada in 1866. In that version, the writer chose the name from the keeping of his bar tab: "When he came in there and took them on tick, Johnny used to sing out to the bar-keeper, who carried a lump of chalk in his weskit pocket and kept the score, 'mark twain,' whereupon the barkeeper would score two drinks to Sam's account—and so it was, d'ye see, that he came to be called Mark Twain."

MOVERS AND SHAKERS

Readers of Twain's fiction may also not realize the riverboat derivation of the last name of his fictional creation Tom Sawyer. Since the eighteenth century, SAWYER has indicated a floating tree or log that poses problems for boating; in 1790, a river traveler noted, "Another dangerous obstruction is a tree becoming undermined and falling into the river . . . the limbs wear off, and the body keeps sawing up and down with great force, rising frequently several feet above the water, and then sinking as much below. These are called sawyers, and often cause accidents to unsuspecting navigators."

A number of America's other travel terms predate the for-mation of the United States. In the 1700s, for instance, TRAV-ELING MINISTER was introduced as the term for any itinerant preacher, before the regular routes were established for the CIRCUIT RIDER, a term that entered the language almost a century later.

Joshua Hempstead recorded a 1741 entry in his diary that "Traveling ministers . . . in Some places promote the withdrawing from the Settled ministers & Set up Separate meetings." The itinerant preacher Francis Asbury shortened the term to TRAVELER; he wrote in 1813 about "the increase . . . in preachers seventy-nine; but of these there are only thirty-three travellers." Three decades later, a survey in Indiana suggested the rapid growth of religion in America with a census showing "more than 2,000 local preachers, besides the traveling ministers."

In the 1840s, the novelist James Fenimore Cooper introduced a traveling use of LINE, often used as the plural LINES, as the term to mark the western frontier, particularly the ever-expanding boundary intruding upon Native American land. A decade later, the crossing of the Rocky Mountains was described by a traveler as proceeding "over twelve miles of magnificent country to the Line: I don't mean the great globular girdle . . . but the line of demarcation between the pale-face and the Indian: the extreme margin of civilization." As more and more Indian land was taken away, the line moved farther westward until that sense of the term disappeared from the language.

ON THE WAGON

Also unfamiliar in today's lexicon of travel terms is OREGON TRAILER, not a mobile home but a follower of the main trail west. Named for the early nineteenth century route leading westward from Independence, Missouri, the Oregon Trail moved emigrants into the Oregon country. A 1949 magazine in Omaha described one of the many difficulties faced by these travelers a century before: "Oregon Trailers of the 1850s often found Nebraska herbage so depleted by buffalo hordes that their plodding ox teams had to be fed hay and grain brought in the wagons."

The cost of travel, even by wagon, was always a necessary consideration. George Washington used the British term WAGONAGE in 1757 when he wrote of the money charged for such travel: "The amount of waggonage and other charges of transporting these provisions . . . will exceed the whole cost of the provisions." Since the 1840s, an assembly of wagons took on the label of WAGON TRAIN.

Westward travel also developed in the language a range of terms for movement by wagon. The name of the PRAIRIE SCHOONER, celebrated for its shiplike appearance, was used in the 1840s, followed three decades later by PRAIRIE CLIPPERS. A simpler PRAIRIE WAGON appeared by 1855 and was described shortly after the Civil War as "smaller in size, frailer in build, without a floor, with very bad springs, and with canvas blinds for windows."

The CONESTOGA WAGON's name derived from the location of its original construction in the Conestoga Valley, Pennsylvania, and the STOGIE as a cigar came from a clipping of "Conestoga" (that foot-long cigar was supposedly the favorite of the wagoners who drove the Conestoga over long distances). By the 1890s, the strong wagons made in Pennsylvania were also known as ARKS; in 1891, an elderly writer recalled the signs of westward movement during the 1830s: "Almost any day from April to October, might have been seen passing . . . a dozen in line of Pennsylvania Arks (wagons) or 'Prairie Schooners,' so called from their rising stem and stern, with great canvas covers, sustained by curved top hoops."

As transportation needs became more sophisticated, so did the types and names of these vehicles. In her 1869 novel *Little Women,* Louisa May Alcott became the first writer to mention the BEACH WAGON, an open wagon with two or more seats. A generation later, DEAD WAGON was introduced to identify the wagon that carried corpses to the undertaker. As early as 1908, a vehicle that provided sightseeing tours was identified as a RUBBERNECK WAGON.

In the twentieth century, abstaining from alcohol became widely known as being ON THE WAGON. That wagon term, however, began as the synonymous ON THE WATER-CART. In a turn-of-the-century novel, one character suggests drinking to another: "I wanted to git him some whisky, but he shuck his head. 'I'm on the water-cart,' sez he."

In contrast, falling off that water-cart (or "water wagon") became a modern metaphor for a return to drinking alcohol. Both possibilities, however, were reflected upon in a 1906 sentiment: "It is better to have been on and off the Wagon than never to have been on at all."

CROSS WORDS

Being able to cross the country proved a challenge that also led to new words.

Harper's Magazine in 1853 introduced into print the adjective TRANSCONTINENTAL, writing about a proposed "company, embracing the wealthiest of New York capitalists, to construct a trans-continental railroad." Mark Twain extended a figurative sense to that lengthy adjective in his 1889 novel, *A Connecticut Yankee in King Arthur's Court:* "She pulled out . . . and got her train fairly started on one of those horizonless trans-continental sentences of hers."

The prefix TRANS- traveled well. In 1825, a question about the unity of the Union introduced a term for the states west of the Allegheny Mountains: "Why should the trans-Allegany States have remained united with those on the Atlantic, when the mountains rendered all profitable intercourse between them impracticable?" A bird-watching text in 1831 moved the trans- usage farther westward: "In the trans-Mississippian territories of the United States, the burrowing owl resides."

The Missouri River was linguistically crossed by an 1870 reference to "the trans-Missouri plains," and by 1935 TRANS-SIERRAN was in use for crossing the Sierra Nevada.

Crossing the Great Plains to the Far West became known by the modifier OVERLAND. The expression "Overland Mail" was used for the postal service across land between St. Louis and San Francisco, with stagecoaches employed in the delivery starting in 1858. This system of using wagons was replaced in 1869 after the completion of the transcontinental railroad.

Water travel originated other terms. For instance, the appropriately named WEIGH LOCK was mentioned in 1833 for a canal lock for weighing or ascertaining the tonnage of barges. (Today's highway version of that water term would be the truck WEIGH STATION.) Less obvious was the river use of the name TEXAS, with or without a capital *T*, which was a steamboat term for officer quarters constructed on the hurricane deck. Mitford M. Mathews expressed the doubtful origins of that riverboat usage: "The commonly accepted view is that the custom arose of naming staterooms on Mississippi steamers after states, whereupon the officers' room, being the largest, was named after the largest state. The evidence at hand is not sufficient to substantiate this, or any other explanation of the origin of this application of the term."

THE ROAD TAKEN

The distance traveled and conditions for the trip led to other expressions. A short distance, more widely known as "a stone's throw," took the name of SQUIRREL'S JUMP in the 1830s; an 1838 issue of *Knickerbocker Magazine* asked, "Have you ever been as far as a squirrel's jump from it?"

A small obstruction or depression in the road gained the designation of THANK-YOU-MA'AM. The poet Henry Wadsworth

Longfellow explained that usage in 1849: "The driver called them thank-you-ma'ams, because they made everybody bow."

Travel by foot also produced new terms. The popular western term TENDERFOOT was perhaps a back-formation from the adjective "tenderfooted"; that earlier English adjective for "sensitive or timid" appeared in 1842 in an Illinois newspaper: "When this was proposed, upon the stump, in the late canvass, how many tenderfooted, used like GREENHORN for a newcomer, democrats united with the Whigs, to ridicule the idea, and prove it Demagoguism!" Since the middle of the nineteenth century, the noun has referred to any inexperienced or youthful arrival in the West. An 1849 use in California was reported by *American Speech:* "We saw a man in Sacramento when we were on our way here, who was a tenderfoot, or rawheel, or whatever you call 'em, who struck a pocket of gold." The transferred sense of the 1880s no longer applied only to people; in 1887, *Scribner's Magazine* reported that "PILGRIM and tenderfoot were formerly applied almost exclusively to newly imported cattle."

More jocular were such terms as ANT KILLERS in reference to the feet and ANKLE EXPRESS in reference to walking. In Kentucky during the 1840s, a man was accused of stepping on a long-tailed cat; the man responded, "Well let hir keep hir tail clar of my ant killers!" A Texas writer in 1920 referred to a long walk taken decades before by saying, "I took the ankle express for my home." Still heard as a term for the feet is CLOD-HOPPERS, a variant of another slang term identified in the 1880s as an Americanism, CLOD-CRUSHERS. A slang dictionary explained "clod-crushers" as "an epithet used by Americans to describe the large feet which they believe to be the characteristics of Englishwomen as compared with those of their own country." The similiar "clod-hopper," originally found in England in the seventeenth century as a term for a rustic yokel, led the comedian Red Skelton to create the comic character known as Clem Cadiddlehopper.

Travel westward, however, was not always successful. Go-
BACK, for example, was the term for one returning eastward
after a failure to succeed in the West. An unsympathetic use
of that term appeared in the *Rocky Mountain News* in 1859:
"Farewell to the gobacks; they have had their day, and soon
will be forgotten." Reports of poor mining results, known also
as PIKE'S PEAK HUMBUG, caused many would-be miners to
return home, and an 1884 work on Colorado commented,
"The army of go-backs grew greater than the advancing host,
and they did many a tale unfold, declaring there was not a
thimbleful of gold in the country." Farmers picked up the term
in GO-BACK LAND, for farmland that had been cultivated but
was then allowed to return to wilderness.

Travelers found that STATION-KEEPER was used in the
early nineteenth century for anybody who maintained a station along the Oregon Trail. Later in that century, though, the
same term referred to one in charge of a refuge for slaves trying to flee north.

In the 1830s the UNDERGROUND RAILROAD was developed
to assist the fugitive slaves. A New York newspaper reported
in 1842 that "We passed 26 prime slaves to the land of freedom last week. . . . All went by the underground railroad."
Harriet Tubman's secret transportation network was known
also as the UNDERGROUND RAILWAY; an 1856 description
talked of "the underground railway. It consists of persons who
are prepared to hide such fugitives during the day, and assist
them on, from one to another, under cover of the night."

A third term was simply the UNDERGROUND, used in the
1852 novel, *Uncle Tom's Cabin* by Harriet Beecher Stowe.
The African-American orator Frederick Douglass, however,
expressed his displeasure with the widespread use of the term
in his 1845 autobiography: "I have never approved of the
very public manner in which some of our western friends have
conducted what they call the underground railroad, but

which, I think, by their open declarations, has been made most emphatically the upperground railroad."

Long after "lines" was used for the frontier, the railroad's popularity led to phrases still in popular use: RIGHT SIDE OF THE TRACKS and WRONG SIDE OF THE TRACKS. Predating the Depression, these terms were explained by a writer in 1929: "In most commuting towns of any recognized worth, there are always two sides of which the tracks serve as a line of demarcation. There is the right side and the wrong side. Translated into terms of modern American idealism, this means, the rich side and the side that hopes to be rich." The terms have been used since the Depression, particularly to derogate anybody born on the "wrong side" of those tracks.

THE NEW FRONTIER

America's air travel led to the growing popularity of another phrase: PUSH THE ENVELOPE. Test pilots in the 1940s used ENVELOPE for the limits of performance for any aircraft; that aeronautical term dates back to 1901 and indicates the perfect inflation of an airship or hot-air balloon, based on an earlier envelope in mathematics for the outer boundary of a group of curves. In the 1979 book *The Right Stuff*, Tom Wolfe explained the verb's significance to astronauts: " 'Pushing the outside,' probing the outer limits, of the envelope seemed to be the great challenge and satisfaction of flight test." By the late 1980s the expression was being used to refer to pushing any type of boundaries.

Space, known alliteratively as the "final frontier" since the 1960s, continues to fuel the American desire to go beyond, to push the existing envelope. In July 1997, the first spacecraft landed on Mars. Its telling name was PATHFINDER, a noun coined by James Fenimore Cooper as the title for his 1840 novel. The term became a nickname for the explorer John C. Frémont, known in the later nineteenth century as "the Pathfinder of the West." A British book about Kansas in 1857 described a determined character as being "full of cool courage and determination as the Western pathfinder is."

A year later, the word was used jocularly in a political put-down of Philip C. Schuyler, who the *New York Tribune* reported "is now repudiated by the Republican party all over Kansas, and couldn't be elected Pathfinder in his own town." (The *Tribune* writer was alluding to PATHMASTER, an 1842 noun for an elected official who keeps up the local roads; today's version of a lowly officeholder would be "dog catcher.")

Upon the Mars Pathfinder was a mobile machine for gathering information. That machine is known as a "rover," long a standard name for a dog and used since the 1870s as the nickname for a resident of Colorado. This particular rover took the name of SOJOURNER, a Standard English term for "traveler." The name's distinguished American lineage includes the advent of the abolitionist Sojourner Truth, an African-American who was born a slave called Isabella and who adopted her more memorable name in 1843 when she became an evangelist; her message of equal rights, spread from town to town, was frequently punctuated in her speeches with the reminder, "And ain't I a woman?"

Not all modern movers have celebrated the speed of American travel. The late CBS commentator Charles Kuralt, famed for his reports in *On the Road,* was concerned about mixing recklessness and restlessness. "Thanks to the Interstate Highway System," he observed in 1985, "it is . . . possible to travel across the country from coast to coast without seeing anything."

It was a contemporary of Mark Twain, however, who best expressed the pleasurable possibilities of a restless lifestyle. Charles Dudley Warner, the editor and essayist who died in

1900, noted the simple truth that "In order to travel one must have a home, and one that is loved and pulling a little at the heart strings all the while; for the best thing about traveling is going home."

Directional Signals

ABOUT EAST an early-nineteenth-century New England expression for "all right" or "O.K."

DOWN EAST a Maine expression, in use since the 1820s, for that northeastern state and the Maritime Provinces of Canada

SOUTHLAND a term used by the 1840s for the southern states and by the turn of the century for the southern part of California

WESTERN AMERICANISH an 1850s adjective to describe frontier life or manners

NORTH-ENDER an obsolete 1860s term for a resident of the northern part of Boston

SOUTH END a nineteenth-century colloquialism for the buttocks; in 1873, Mark Twain wrote, "He bent stooping forward, with his back sagged and his South end sticking out far"

BLUE NORTHER an 1870s term for a violent storm in which a fiercely cold wind from the north blows across Texas and the rest of the Southwest

NORTH-WESTER an 1884 noun for a tall tale originating in the Pacific Northwest

WOOLLY WEST an 1890s shortening of "wild and woolly West" as a colloquialism for the lawlessness of life on the frontier

EAST SIDESE a twentieth-century colloquialism for the method of speaking heard on Manhattan's East Side, used in 1911 to report that " 'gatts' is East Sidese for 'pistols' "

CHAPTER 15

EXAGGERATION

*M*ark Twain knew the ways of Southerners almost as well as he knew the twists of the Mississippi. To them, the Civil War was known as "the War," and its effect lasted long beyond the 1865 surrender. "In the South," Twain once commented, "The War is what A.D. is elsewhere; they date from it. All day long you hear things 'placed' as having happened since the War; or 'du'in' the War,' or 'befo' the War.' "

It was in the midst of the Civil War that the sixteenth president of the United States began to draft what would become his second annual message to Congress. On the first day of December in 1862, he wanted to convey in language that could not be misunderstood what he perceived of the American experiment. The expression that Abraham Lincoln chose was deliberate: "We shall nobly save or meanly lose the last, best hope of earth." For that uplifting phrase, Lincoln may have looked to the first Inaugural Address of Thomas Jefferson. In that 1801 speech, Jefferson looked to America's new system of government as "the world's best hope."

Such idealistic visions are often depicted in rhetoric by

using *hyperbole,* a fifteenth-century term indicating exaggeration for effect. The American language in particular has long been filled with hyperbolic terms, including this hype of "hope," to stretch and exaggerate meanings as a way to excite the imaginations of readers and listeners. HYPE, a twentieth-century Americanism that may have come from a back-formation of "hyperbole," pointed the path that took America from tall talk to the commercialese heard across the nation in modern times.

NAME TAG

The tall talk of the nineteenth century helped expand the volume of America's vocabulary. As the main proponent of tall talk, Davy Crockett lent his name to the practice of those trying to imitate or outperform his frontier image. In 1834, two years before Crockett's death at the Alamo, a New York newspaper urged another frontiersman to become more subdued: "Stop, stop, you OUT-CROCKETT Davy Crockett." That usage in turn alludes to a similar coinage by William Shakespeare, who wrote in *Hamlet* that a character's overacting "out-Herods Herod."

Other names were used in the early days of America to form words and phrases. Dr. Sylvester Graham, a reformer of the American diet who died in 1851, lent his name to a dietetic flour of whole wheat; that name remains familiar from the slightly sweet baked product known as the GRAHAM CRACKER, first mentioned in print in 1882. As a strict advocate of dieting, he offered a rigid system known as "Grahamism," and those who went beyond those guidelines were said in the 1830s to OUT-GRAHAM GRAHAM, which today would probably be labeled an eating disorder. "A married woman is exhibiting herself at Montreal," a Boston newspaper reported in 1834, "who for abstemiousness outGrahams

Graham 'all the world to nothing.' She has subsisted for two years past on nothing—saving milk or tea. "

HEAP BIG

Some terms borrowed from British English received remarkable use in America. The adjective HANDSOME, for example, began in Middle English with the sense of "easy to use," but its use spread more broadly in the United States than it did in England. A British visitor reported in 1837 that "The Americans use the word handsome much more extensively than we do: saying that Webster made a handsome speech in the Senate; that a lady talks handsomely (eloquently), that a book sells handsomely. A gentleman asked me on the Catskill Mountain, whether I thought the sun handsomer there than at New York."

The use of HEAP as a modifier, on the other hand, was exclusively American, as in the phrase "heap big." Although that wording was said to come from native speech, it may have been from settlers imitating Indian language. An 1848 issue of *Blackwell's Magazine* made this usage seem commonplace in Indian talk: "An Indian is always a 'heap' hungry or thirsty—loves a 'heap'—is a 'heap' brave—in fact, 'heap' is tantamount to very much."

The origin of the encompassing SHEBANG remains uncertain. This Americanism first appeared during the Civil War as a term for a hut or temporary shelter. The poet Walt Whitman wrote in 1862 of being "among the groups around the fires, in their shebang enclosures of bushes." This sense may have resulted from the older Irish noun *shebeen,* referring to an unlicensed place that sells alcohol. In 1869, Mark Twain introduced the slang sense of "business" or "thing," as in THE WHOLE SHEBANG, and two years later, the word "shebang" was in use at Yale to mean "rooms" or "place of abode," as well as being a college term for a theatrical presentation in a public hall.

Other terms to imply size or power came from older English terms. The British dialect verb "scrouge" has been used for "to crowd" since 1755. In the United States originated the noun SCROUGER, for somebody or something of impressive size or ability. This synonym for SCREAMER was employed among other names to identify rowdy boat workers; a Virginia newspaper noted in 1822 that "bargemen . . . are divided into classes, such as Tuscaloosa Roarers, Alabama Screamers, Cahawba Scrougers, and the like gentle names." The British "toad" also lent itself to an 1877 American expression for the person of most importance: BIGGEST TOAD IN THE PUDDLE.

THUNDERER, also introduced in Britain, became a popular American term for something big or exceptional. A panther, according to *Harper's Magazine* in 1857, "was a thunderer, I tell ye." Fifteen years later, the term appeared in a (literal) fish story: "Dick talked and vociferated, slashed his rod in the water, hooked a 'thunderer' and let him get away." The great orator Daniel Webster used THUNDER itself in 1838 to refer to a strong statement or argument: "Another will exclaim, 'That won't do; that's not my thunder.' " Two years earlier, the extended oath of THUNDERATION was roared.

HORSE PLAY

Animal terms were often used for exaggeration. Frontiersman and boatmen, particularly in Kentucky, were described as HALF HORSE AND HALF ALLIGATOR. In his 1809 history of New York, Washington Irving added yet another half in noting "that the back-wood-men of Kentucky are styled half man, half horse, and half alligator by the settlers on the Mississippi, and held accordingly in great respect and abhorrence." As the term moved westward, more animal imagery was injected, such as "with a cross of the wild cat" or "a little touched with the snapping turtle." In 1832, a boatman who "was accustomed to designate himself as 'half horse, half alligator, and a little of the steamboat,' he ever afterwards added 'a small sprinkling of an earthquake' to the former ingredients."

Davy Crockett had identified the phrase as an Arkansas attribute in his 1834 autobiography. But in a nineteenth-century ballad by Samuel Woodworth, "The Hunters of Kentucky," was the observation that "Kentucky boys are Alligator-horses"; that song celebrated the Kentuckians who fought under General John Coffee in the 1815 Battle of New Orleans.

The horse was particularly popular in American expressions. A device for making noise was called a HORSE FIDDLE, explained in *Dialect Notes* in 1907 as an Arkansas term for "a tin can with a resin-smeared thread passed through a hole punctured at the bottom. Pulling the string produces ear-splitting noises." The name appears in print a century earlier, but any attempt to determine its origin would be discouraged by an 1872 comment that "It is called in the West a horse-fiddle, because it is so unlike either a horse or a fiddle."

By the middle of the nineteenth century, HORSE RESTAURANT was the exaggerated term for a livery stable. Caused by animals and people, pollution in America's cities was decried as early as 1824, when a newspaper in Albany, New York, worried about filthy streets with "such savoury exhalations as may be supposed to arise from skunk's purgatory, if there is such a place, and we know of no reason why there should not be as well as a HORSE-HEAVEN." By the late 1880s, that horse phrase was capitalized as a region of the Northwest where cayuse ponies once roamed. Fences able to hold horses as well as other animals were called HORSE HIGH. Western courts in 1873 elaborated the order that an adequate fence by law would be "horse-high, bull-strong, and pig-tight." With horses also known by the Southernism CREATURES or the variant CRITTERS, a unit of cavalry was encompassed as a CRITTER COMPANY by the end of the Civil War.

The measure of size or importance relied on another equine term first used in the nineteenth century. The phrase ONE-HORSE, as in the 1853 reference to "One Horse Town," suggested that something was small or insignificant. A small farm, for instance, has long been described with this phrase, because the property could be worked with only a single horse.

Encompassing terms in America reached to cover ALL NATURE or ALL OUTDOORS. An 1819 issue of the *Massachusetts Spy* used the former term to refer to everybody: "Father and I have just returned from the balloon—all nature was there, and more too." To surpass or excel everything else was TO BEAT ALL NATURE, first used in 1825. The similar "all outdoors" stood for the entire world. AS BIG AS ALL OUTDOORS, still in common use to describe a generous person's heart, dates back to 1825. Perhaps most popular was ALL-CREATION, used throughout the nineteenth century as a term for "everybody or everything." Reinforced with a verb like "beat" or "lick," the term became a strong challenge; in 1891, a slang dictionary defined the American usage of TO BEAT (or LICK) ALL CREATION as "to overpower; excel; surpass; to be incomparable."

SIZE COUNTS

Inflation of job titles has also led to exaggerations in America's language. In the middle of the nineteenth century, almost any person employed by a college was given the grandiose title of "Professor" by the students. An 1851 collection of college terms identified that worker with the honorary moniker PROFESSOR OF DUST AND ASHES, first recorded in 1847, as "a title sometimes jocosely given by students to the person who has the care of their rooms."

Even the business of cutting hair was given elevated prestige in the language. BARBERSHOP, for instance, appeared in British English in an isolated example in 1579, but the term was apparently forgotten and then re-formed in the United States in 1832. Its continued importance during the twentieth century was underlined by a comment in a 1947 newspaper from Duluth, Minnesota: "More fish are 'caught' in a barber shop on an average winter afternoon than are taken in many lakes all summer." As a bastion of male bonding, this shop was also known as a BARBER HOUSE later in the nineteenth century. A more grandiloquent term for the same business was SHAVING SALOON, dating back to 1846. The barber himself was raised to the level of TONSORIALIST a few decades later— just as a bartender became known as a MIXOLOGIST—but not even that title proved adequate. In 1875, the same businessman became known by a grander phrase: "Now, the men mostly go to a TONSORIAL ARTIST (formerly a barber)."

Out of mining hyperbole of a century ago came today's use of GRASSROOTS for something basic or fundamental. Miners used GRASSROOTS for the soil directly below the surface of the ground, and a hyperbolic writer raved in an 1876 work about the Black Hills that "Gold is found almost everywhere, in the bars, in the gravel and sand of the beds, even in the 'grass roots.' "

H. L. Mencken in *The American Language* noted the difficulties of finding the origin of the term's political application; in 1945, Mencken wrote that "The late Dr. Frank H. Vizetelly told me in 1935 that he had been informed that grass-roots, in the verb-phrase TO GET DOWN TO GRASS-ROOTS, was in use in Ohio circa 1885, but he could never track down a printed record of it, and neither could I." The voters at this level who are said to wield political power became identified by 1947 with the American folk expression of GRASS ROOTERS.

Among American folk comparisons, perhaps the best known is KNEE-HIGH TO A GRASSHOPPER. That term, used most often in referring to a remote past, may point to somebody's youth, as in "back when your grandfather was knee-high to a grasshopper." The comparison, though, did not begin with "grasshopper," although that insect has seen widespread usage in the language. The GRASSHOPPER BATTLE, for instance, denoted native fighting in which the Delaware tribe defeated the Shawnees; this deadly combat was alleged in the 1870s to have started with a quarrel among Indian children about who possessed a certain grasshopper. A Southernism of the 1820s turned the term around into the jocular HOPPER-GRASS.

In 1814, the comparative phrase for size was "knee-high to a TOAD," and a decade later a New York newspaper used a variant MOSQUITO spelling for "knee-high to a musquitoe." A Louisville paper in 1833 offered "knee-high to a FROG," in 1911 came "knee-high to a DUCK," and *Harper's Magazine* reduced the comparison even more in 1947 with "Fatigue was gone forever when, knee-high to NOTHING, I caught my first trout." An 1851 issue of the *Democratic Review,* however, was the publication that first offered the current form: "You pretend to be my daddies; some of you who are not knee-high to a grasshopper!"

FARM FRESH

A comparative term for value still familiar from the American frontier is SMALL POTATOES. Back in 1831, a Boston newspaper used this British term to indicate insignificance or triviality: "When a person is guilty of a mean action, or takes much

pains to make himself ridiculous, it is often said in relation to
the circumstance, 'small potatoes—rather small potatoes, and
few in a hill.' " In 1948, the term expressed the magnitude of
h "The $7 billion was of course pretty
ared to the vast inflationary borrowings
nent."

o being used attributively as a put-down
Orleans publication addressed "Creole
ers, small potato readers," and an 1896
politics mentioned an editor's "habit of
r Seward as his 'small potato highness,'
as 'a galvanized squash,' " using another

wever, is the exaggerated reverse of small
ltural opposite of that paltry produce be-
letters to form SOME PUMPKINS. In 1846,
pplied to both people and things, even
itself meant "a chump" before the Revo-
ed to the insult of PUMPKIN HEAD. A 1781
ticut reported that "New Haven is cele-
iven the name of pumpkin-heads to all the
t originated from the Blue Laws, which en-
have his hair cut round by a cap. When
had, they substituted the hard shell of a

ion of "some," respect became attached to
as applied to anybody of importance or con-
dly competition among acquaintances in the
tains was reported in 1848: "The contest
efforts to excel each other in complimenting
the climax of the argument seemed to be that
Mr. Clingman was not 'some pumpkins' but 'Pumpkins.' "
That same year, a letter from New Orleans appeared in a New
York newspaper favoring a politician who "is some pumpkins,

and will do the needful in the office line if he is elected." From the South and West, this imprecise means of American measure spread throughout the country.

Throughout the twentieth century, the language has inflated other words and phrases. A trailer park, for instance, is now a MOBILE HOME COMMUNITY, just as an ambulance now has the emergency designation of ADVANCED LIFE SUPPORT VEHICLE. The medical use of "clinic" has given way in many cities to WELLNESS CENTER, while the Food Lion grocery chain renamed those in charge of produce as PERISHABLE MANAGERS, despite the deadly implications of that inflation. Even simple take-out meals are now supposed to be called HOME MEAL REPLACEMENTS.

Inflated oaths as well have long been part of America's language. In the frontier memoir *Little House on the Prairie,* first published in 1935, Laura Ingalls Wilder recalled an 1870s episode in which her Pa struggled to handle an unwilling cow: " 'Now, by the GREAT HORN SPOON, I'll milk her!' he said."

That oath referred to the "horn spoon," also known as the "horned spoon" or "horn," used by miners as they worked. The crude implement, primarily a spoon or scoop of horn to test washings by prospectors, was mentioned by an 1869 miner in Apache country: "There was as nice a little deposit of pure gold in the bottom of the horn as ever I saw taken at random from any mine." The euphemistic oath appeared in a song printed in 1842: "He vow'd by the great horn spoon / He'd give them a licking, and that pretty soon." A variant term, based on the same mining device, was "by the sacred horn spoon," but that phrase never achieved the popularity of "by the great horn spoon."

GREAT also appeared in such place names as "the Great West" and "the Great White Way." By 1832, "Great West" was in use for the western territory, and as long ago as World War I, there was already concern expressed about "the vanishing romance of the Great West." William Clark, famed for the Lewis and Clark expedition of the early 1800s, used the modifier form when he wrote after first seeing the Pacific in 1805 that it "is now 24 days since we arrived in sight of the Great Western Ocean." In New York City, "the Great White Way" identified the section of Broadway close to Times Square and received its name from being brightly illuminated at night. "Start at Fifty-ninth Street and walk down what the Manhattanese call The Great White Way," *The Saturday Evening Post* invited its readers in 1909.

The same modifier has appeared in dozens of other American expressions. James Knox Polk, the eleventh president of the United States, made a diary note in 1845 about meeting with Indians: "In their talk they addressed the President as their GREAT FATHER, and Mrs. Polk as their GREAT MOTHER." Other aboriginal Americans, however, disavowed those phrases, sometimes pointing to the sun itself as the "father." By the twentieth century, GREAT WHITE FATHER was reported as another term for the president in Indian speech, although the native use of "father" was found in 1904 to have extended to other leaders: "The expression was transferred from the French Governor of Canada to the King of France, from the King of France to the King of Great Britain, and from the King of Great Britain to the President of the United States." The specific application to the president was, of course, reinforced by the nicknaming of George Washington "the father of his country."

Great Weight

GREAT ECLIPSE a New England term for the solar eclipse that occurred in 1806 (a new wine imported into Boston arrived at the same time and was known as "eclipse wine"); not to be confused with the DARK DAY in May 1780 when an unexplained darkness descended across New England

GREAT KNIFE a 1791 term used by Indians to designate an American in contrast to an Englishman

GREAT WATER an Indian expression used in the early 1800s for the Atlantic Ocean and later, in the plural "great waters," for the Mississippi River

GREAT AMERICAN DESERT an 1834 phrase for the Great Plains, which at one time was considered a desert

GREAT BUG a person of importance; an 1840 term that was an inflation of the earlier phrase "big bug"

GREAT METROPOLIS an 1846 term for New York City to emphasize the city's size

GREAT TREE an 1855 term in California for the sequoia, also known as the giant redwood, or the "big tree" of the bald cypress family that may grow almost three hundred feet tall

GREAT DIVIDE an 1860s term for the Great Continental Divide, the Rocky Mountain watershed that also serves as a metaphorical term for death in "crossing the great divide"

GREAT SNAKES! an exclamation of surprise or dismay; colloquialism dating back to World War I

GREAT DEPRESSION the financial depression that struck the economy of the United States in 1929, with its economic effects felt for almost a decade

CHAPTER 16

INDIGNATION

$\mathcal{T}$he anger level is rising in America, and our words are not immune.

"It was John Witherspoon who coined the word AMERI-CANISM," noted the essayist H. L. Mencken in 1918, "and at once the English guardians of the sacred vessels began employing it as a general synonym for vulgarism and barbarism." Two centuries later, angry Americans proclaimed themselves members of MADD, "Mothers Against Drunk Driving," just one of the countless protests of modern American life.

From witchcraft to Watergate, America has long weighed in with words that conjure a nation of indignation.

A colonial witness to the witchcraft at Salem Village in April 1692 recorded a memorable visit to the home of the Reverend Samuel Parris: "When I was there, his Kinswoman, Abigail Williams (about 12 years of age), had a grievous fit; she was at first hurryed with Violence to and fro in the room, . . . sometimes makeing as if she would fly, stretching up her arms as high as she could, and crying 'Whish, Whish,

Whish!' several times. . . . After that, she run to the Fire, and begun to throw Fire Brands, about the house."

WHISH as an interjection is British in origin (the verb form originated in the sixteenth century), and unfortunately the New World imported more than words from the Old World. Fear of witchcraft was among the notions that colonists carried with them from the Continent, leading to the execution of twenty people in the colony of Massachusetts by the end of 1692. In one of the most shameful episodes of early American history, nineteen victims were hanged on Gallows Hill outside of Salem, and one man was pressed to death beneath rocks; despite popular folklore to the contrary, none was burned at the stake.

In the 1956 book *The Witchcraft of Salem Village,* the American novelist Shirley Jackson wrote hauntingly of the sad irony behind the score of deaths. "Not one person," she observed, "who confessed to practicing witchcraft was executed. The persons executed were those who insisted upon their innocence."

Shirley Jackson herself, however, apparently believed in magic. When she became peeved with her publisher Alfred A. Knopf, she is said to have fashioned an image of Knopf in wax and stuck into the leg a sharp pin. That weekend, on a skiing trip, Knopf broke his leg.

OUTER LIMITS

American angst has created a readiness to argue about almost anything. Radio and television talk shows are crowded with angry expressions on subjects that our ancestors never negotiated, from the H.M.O. (Health Maintenance Organization) to the G.M.O. (Genetically Modified Organism) and even DESIGNER FAMILIES (a current coinage for manipulating pregnancies to produce children of a sex chosen in advance).

Anger and indignation erupt most forcefully, however, from Americans who find themselves on the outside looking in.

OUTSIDER, for example, has been in use since 1800. The noun refers to a person who does not belong to a particular group. (British use of the same word indicates somebody who enters a competition but is not expected to win.) In 1848, the American outsider became politicized in meaning, specifically referring to somebody who is unconnected with the two major political divisions; back then, those forces were the Whigs and the Locofocos. "With the outsiders of all descriptions," editorialized the *New York Mirror* in June of 1848, ". . . the nomination of General Taylor is equally a cause of delight." In today's usage, that outsider has become an INDEPENDENT.

Also coming out in the 1840s was the term COME-OUTER. This expression, according to John Bartlett, became a New England term for anybody choosing to leave organized religion for independent faith. "They have no creed," states the entry in Bartlett's dictionary of Americanisms, "believing that every one should be left free to hold such opinions on religious subjects as he pleases, without being held accountable for the same to any human authority." When politics took in the same term, "come-outer" referred to any person who favored political reform.

For more than a century, IN has been used to describe the political party currently holding sway, and OUT refers to the party that is out of power. "This election," said Herbert Hoover in 1932, "is not a mere shift from the Ins to the Outs. It means deciding the directions our nation will take over a century to come."

OUTRIDER began in British usage in the sixteenth century. The first outrider was an attendant mounted on a horse, and the sense that evolved in the Old West also referred to a hired helper on horseback. At home on the range, the western outrider worked as a cowboy who traveled wherever the boss needed him to check for trouble. Unlike the LINE RIDER who specialized in watching the line or boundary of an area, the outrider covered the entire ranch or range as the boss directed.

Out of the film industry have appeared many of this century's "out" terms. Since 1902, for instance, OUTTAKE has been part of the language, first as the term for a vent and then for a bit of film or recorded material that is edited from a completed work. FADE-OUT came into the American vocabulary by the time of World War I, when it was employed for the gradual decrease in a visual image at the end of a movie sequence. (ACT OUT, referring to childish behavior, also began with a theatrical sense, and often leads to TIME-OUT, a 1926 expression for a break in activity.)

The current decade's use of "outsider" covers a trend in contemporary art that emphasizes the creations of an untrained or unschooled artist from outside the mainstream. Growing out of what was called "folk art" earlier in the century, OUTSIDER ART designates works of primitive, raw visions, often captured in untraditional materials that range from bones or bottlecaps to aluminum cans or other items of refuse. Anne H. Soukhanov, the "Word Watch" columnist for *The Atlantic,* noted that outsider artists "are often country folk, the elderly, the very young, or sometimes the mentally ill."

Modern "out" phrases range from expressions of explicitness (OUT OF THE CLOSET, based on a 1950s term for sexual liberation) to indications of ignorance (OUT OF THE LOOP, a 1985 phrase for denying awareness or guilt). As forms of protest, the 1840s WALKOUT led to the 1951 SICKOUT.

Not every modern-sounding expression is as recent as it may seem. Consider the complimentary comment OUT OF SIGHT, usually run together in hippie-era slang as OUTTA SIGHT. The phrase has New York origins in the middle of the nineteenth century. By the 1890s, it made its literary debut, when it appeared in *Maggie: A Girl of the Streets,* a novel by

Stephen Crane. "I'm stuck on her shape," Crane wrote. "It's outa sight."

GATE KEEPING

The indignation caused by political scandal has been one of the most productive forces behind modern American coinages.

Up till the summer of 1972, the modern American shorthand for political scandal was usually TEAPOT DOME. That name referred to a nine-thousand-acre oilfield in Wyoming. Situated on public land, the Teapot Dome Reserve had been kept in reserve for the navy until the administration of Warren G. Harding. In 1921, Harding authorized the transfer of the oil-rich land to the Department of the Interior, allowing the interior secretary to receive bribes from oil companies wanting to lease the land. The Senate began an investigation in 1923, and the political fallout lasted for years to come, with continued references to the Teapot Dome affair.

Until 1972, WATERGATE was merely the name for a hotel and office complex beside the Potomac River in Washington, D.C. On the night of June 17 that year, however, five men were arrested for breaking into the Democratic National Committee office in that complex, and a story of scandalous proportions began to play itself out on the national stage. By the time Richard Nixon faced almost certain impeachment in 1974, he became the first American president to resign from office.

The language of Watergate became the language of American politics, from BUG and TAP to DIRTY TRICKS and AT THAT POINT IN TIME. The Executive Branch informer who supplied details of White House intrigues was called DEEP THROAT, a pun on "deep background" (meaning that the source would never be identified or even quoted) and *Deep Throat,* an enormously popular pornographic film of 1972.

Deep Throat is still in use to refer to any secret informer.

The name Watergate itself, however, opened a floodgate for the naming of future scandals, the following half a dozen among the most memorable of the late twentieth century:

WINEGATE a French scandal in the 1970s about impurities in fine wines

KOREAGATE a 1976 scandal about the corrupt influencing of Congress by South Korea

IRAQGATE a 1989 scandal involving rocket technology supplied to Iraq

TRAVELGATE a 1993 White House scandal about the president's replacing of travel office staff members with personal friends

FILEGATE a 1997 scandal about the unauthorized review of private FBI files

WHITEWATERGATE a 1990s scandal about financial dealings by Bill and Hillary Clinton in Arkansas before the Clinton presidency

Out of the investigation of that last scandal came ZIPPERGATE, SEXGATE, and MONICAGATE, all public designations of Bill Clinton's affair with a White House intern, and the combining form of -GATE shows no sign of being closed.

STRIKING OUT

"Congress shall make no law," states the First Amendment to the United States Constitution, ". . . abridging the freedom of speech, or of the press; or the right of the people peaceably to assemble, and to petition the Government for a redress of grievances."

Protests as expressions of indignation have spawned their own section of America's vocabulary. A public outcry against unfair policies led to the twentieth century's PROTEST VOTE, the term for casting a ballot against a winning candidate.

More than a century ago, though, protest was registered in what became known as an INDIGNATION MEETING. Back in 1842, a newspaper reported that "We have held an 'indignation meeting' and passed strong resolutions against Mexico." The term remained current as recently as 1948, when *The Saturday Evening Post* observed that "Mothers were holding indignation meetings about the schools."

When action or reform was needed on the local level, a group called an IMPROVEMENT SOCIETY might be formed. "The village improvement societies are signs of the wish to remedy congenital defects of rural communities," *Harper's Magazine* editorialized in 1880.

Sometimes the sweetness of the term belied the anger that the phrase could provoke. SWEETHEART CONTRACT, for instance, sounds innocent enough, but its use at the turn of the twentieth century underscored the close relationship of favored employers to some of the stronger labor unions. By 1900, "sweetheart contract" referred specifically to the unfair favoritism resulting from such closeness, including the practices of paying kickbacks and awarding contracts without open bidding.

Even more colorful is the phrase for a form of protest successfully used by police unions. In use since 1970, the term reflects the color of the police uniform in describing a staged sickout. Its rhyming name: BLUE FLU. Dropping the rhyme but keeping the color has brought us PINK FLU, for an organized sickout of nurses.

ALL THUMBS

Another significant part of the American language is silent: the expressions and gestures known generally as "body language." Even our name for the language, English, has been turned into BODY ENGLISH, or the twisting or movement of the body as if to influence the travel of something already in motion, such as a rolling ball.

These gestures include nods and shrugs, grimaces and curses. An American Indian writer named Zitkala-Sa recalled her childhood at the end of the nineteenth century. She reported a curse that she had watched her mother place upon white settlers: "She sprang to her feet. . . . Raising her right arm forcibly into line with her eye, she threw her whole might into her doubled fist as she shot it vehemently at the strangers. Long she held her outstretched fingers toward the settler's lodge, as if an invisible power passed from them to the evil at which she aimed."

For most Americans, a more familiar gesture today is the "thumbs up" sign, signaling a favorable response. The film critics Siskel and Ebert, for example, show an enthusiastic "thumbs up" for a movie worth seeing and an indignant "thumbs down" for an unfavorable review. A generation of gladiator movies provided the model for that convention, with "thumbs down" intended to signal the death of the fighter.

Oddly, though, the thumb gesturing has reversed itself. A 1601 translation of Pliny's ancient history noted that the Romans would "bend or bow down the thumbes when wee give assent unto a thing, or doe favour any person." As recently as 1887, a biographer of Thomas Carlyle wrote that reviewers of *Sartor Resartus,* Carlyle's major work, "had unanimously turned their thumbs up. 'Sartor,' the publisher acquainted him, 'excites universal disapprobation.' " A 1907 historian of classical antiquity explained the actual practice among the gladiators: " 'Thumbs down' means 'spare him . . .'; the signal for death was 'thumbs up.' "

By the first decade of the twentieth century, these thumb gestures began to reverse their meanings. In 1906, Rudyard Kipling helped that reversal along by writing, "We're finished men—thumbs down against both of us." A World War I diarist commented in 1917 on the "THUMBS UP, Tommy's expression which means 'everything is fine with me.' " Today's gesture of "thumbs up" retains the positive connotation not only in Britain and the United States but also around the world, and the ancient practice of turning thumbs down for encouragement is no longer observed.

In 1936, a publisher rejected the story "Thumbs Up" by F. Scott Fitzgerald. "I thought it was swell," he wrote back to Fitzgerald, "but all the femmes down here said it was horrid. The thumbs, I suppose, were too much for them."

Among scuba divers, the thumb gesture is never used for approbation or disapprobation; a thumbs-up means "ascend," and a thumbs-down means "descend." Instead, the thumb and forefinger are joined in a circle, a more recent gesture now known as the OK SIGN, after the most successful Americanism of them all.

But probably the best known of hand gestures is what we now call THE FINGER. In America this consists of the middle finger jabbed up, with the palm facing inwards; in Great Britain, the index and middle fingers are used, in a perverse inversion of the "*V* for Victory." In both places this is expressive of contempt and hostility.

Many folk stories attempt to explain the origin of the finger—perhaps the best ties it to the Battle of Agincourt in 1415, when Henry V's English longbowmen are said to have taunted the vanquished French with the same two fingers they used to pull back the bowstring. But, like the thumbs up/down, the finger is of ancient origin. In ancient Rome it was known as the *digitus impudicus,* or "rude finger," and reports of it are found in treatises on gestures from the Renaissance. There is even a photograph of a notably ill-mannered baseball player giving the finger in the 1890s. About this time, Funk & Wagnall's *Standard Dictionary* included a definition for "to give one the finger": "To disappoint one . . . ; turn a cold shoulder to one."

GRACE UNDER PRESSURE

Asked to define "guts" in *The New Yorker* in 1929, Ernest Hemingway offered this fearless phrase: "grace under pressure."

America's most graceful speakers and writers have long produced terms to derogate those who promote pessimism. More than a century ago, for instance, CALAMITY HOWLERS became the preferred term for people who predict disaster. A midwestern member of Congress noted in an 1892 *Congressional Record* that "We had some 'calamity howlers' here in Washington as well as in Kansas." This usage won out over such variants as CALAMITY SHOUTERS and CALAMITY PROPHETS, as well as the 1894 proposal of CALAMITYITES.

By the time of the Great Depression, Democrats denounced the negative outlook of the Republicans, who in the mid-1930s were called DISCIPLES OF DESPAIR. A generation later, Clare Boothe Luce was a Republican who turned the tables by calling Democrats TROUBADOURS OF TROUBLE and CROONERS OF CATASTROPHE. The same generation saw the rise of the phrase PROPHETS OF GLOOM AND DOOM, followed in 1993 by Bill Clinton's reference to PREACHERS OF PESSIMISM.

The apex of alienated alliteration, however, appears to have been in the 1970 speeches of Vice President Spiro T. Agnew. The columnist William Safire, then a speechwriter for Agnew, produced NATTERING NABOBS OF NEGATIVISM, which uses the Hindi *nabob* meaning "governor," as well as the extreme "4-H Club—the HOPELESS, HYSTERICAL HYPOCHONDRIACS OF HISTORY." (That exaggerated term for doomsayers is based on the 1926 term for groups of rural young people; the aim of these groups has been to improve "head, heart, hands, and health.")

Mark Twain combined indignation with exaggeration when premature stories of his death began to circulate. In 1897,

Twain visited a cousin in London who was deathly ill, and a mistaken report reached America that the writer himself was dying. A bemused Twain responded to an inquiry from a New York reporter with "the report of my death was an exaggeration." (When Twain retold the story at a later date, he used the more familiar form of the quotation: "Reports of my death have been grossly exaggerated.")

Even more indignant, however, should be Rutherford B. Hayes, the nineteenth president, who died in 1893. The 1998 mail to the Hayes Presidential Center included an invitation for the late president to enjoy a discounted trip to the Caribbean. "Dear Rutherford," the letter begins its offer, adding, "Please do respond promptly so that we may process you."

America's handling of disease and death has not always been comical and has, in fact, produced some memorable metaphors. THE LAST OF PEA TIME, for instance, is a poetic phrase that dates back to 1834; in all its sorrow, the end of the growing season came to represent figuratively a last stage or final period. Feelings of sadness or loss also took on the vivid coloration of having a GRAVEYARD HEART. After the turn of the century, the novelist Gene Stratton-Porter introduced that inspired phrase in *The Girl of the Limberlost,* published in 1909. "When I think of walking off and leaving Freckles, . . . it gives me a graveyard heart."

In American music, few stories about songwriters can equal the pathos and inspiration in the tale that is widely told about Horatio Gates Spafford. Back in the nineteenth century, Spafford was a Chicago newspaperman with a wife and four daughters. In 1873, he said goodbye to his family when they left for a brief European vacation on the ship *Ville du Havre,* and during its Atlantic crossing, the ship sank. Mrs. Spafford was rescued, but the couple's daughters all perished at sea.

Still in deep mourning, Spafford joined his wife in England.

When they sailed back to America on another ship, they were joined by the captain of the *Ville du Havre*. During that return trip, the captain showed Spafford the exact place on the ocean where the earlier ship had gone down with all four of his daughters. Spafford responded to the tragedy by writing the reassuring lyrics for the Protestant hymn "It Is Well with My Soul," which begins with this moving verse:

> When peace, like a river, attendeth my way,
> When sorrows like sea billows roll;
> Whatever my lot, Thou hast taught me to say,
> It is well, it is well with my soul.

America's history, as well as its language, is replete with such stories of perseverance and persistent faith. In 1997, for instance, a library book was returned to Harvard University—hardly a noteworthy occurrence, except that the book had been checked out 233 years ago. (No one knows exactly where this third volume of a *Complete History of England* was for more than two centuries, although optimists have pointed out that its original borrower did save the book from a 1764 fire that destroyed most of Harvard's collection.) The late fee was waived.

The ability to respond with grace instead of indignation, in fact, shows the American character—as well as American wording—at its best. In the nineteenth century, Fanny J. Crosby wrote the lyrics for more than six thousand Protestant hymns, including "Rescue the Perishing" and "Blessed Assurance." This prolific American lyricist could easily have chosen a life of indignation after a doctor's mistreatment had left her blind from infancy.

Good Grief

TO SHOOT YOUR GRANDMOTHER an old New England phrase meaning "to be mistaken or saddened," expressed in the nineteenth century as "You've shot your grandmother"

FROZEN FACE an alliterative century-old phrase for a particularly sad or cold facial expression

FEEL-DAY Depression-era term based on "field day" for a "day to feel good or to overcome sadness"

THE NIAGARA ACT a 1930s expression for crying or weeping, also known as "the sob act"

DRIZZLEPUSS a 1938 depiction of a sad expression, based on the similar "sourpuss"

CRYING a World War II substitute for "single," as in "not a crying cent"

CLOUDBURST a 1940s term for sudden or forceful tears

THE WEEPIES in the last decade, a term for uncontrollable sadness leading to tears, known earlier as "the weeps" and used in British English for tearjerkers

MY BAD a 1990s phrase from African-American usage meaning "It's my fault, or my mistake," "I'm sorry"

GRIEF ROOM a current phrase for the gathering area of relatives and friends awaiting details after a plane crash or similar disaster

CONCLUSION
THE FINAL WORD

*W*hen the spoken word married the silent picture in the film industry's first talkie, Al Jolson uttered six unforgettable words: "You ain't heard nothin' yet, folks!"

America's words, like America's ways, are seldom predictable. Not even the most powerful of politicians can foresee, much less control, what will become the customs or coinages of the United States. Yesterday's language known as "United States" proved itself as far-ranging and alterable as tomorrow's "American" will probably continue to be. The watchword of the American language, as well as its primary characteristic, has always been "independence."

Independence Day itself offers a good example of that unpredictability. This anniversary of adopting the Declaration of Independence was mentioned in a 1791 entry from the diary of Jacob Hiltzheimer, fifteen years after the signing of the document. What remained less clear, however, was the celebration of that holiday.

Back in 1776, the patriot who would become the second president of the United States had his own ideas for saluting the occasion. "It ought to be solemnized," John Adams proposed in a letter to his wife, Abigail, "with Pomp and Parade, with Shews, Games, Sports, Guns, Bells, Bonfires and Illuminations from one End of this Continent to the other from this Time forward forever more." Adams, however, proved less prescient about the date of the celebration, which he predicted would occur every Second of July, not every Fourth. "The Second Day of July," he wrote, "will be the most memorable Epoch, in the History of America. I am apt to believe that it will be celebrated, by succeeding Generations, as the great anniversary Festival."

On July 2, 1776, the Second Continental Congress passed the resolution to seek independence from Britain, with twelve of the thirteen original colonies voting in favor of the motion. (A week afterward, New York added its approval.) Two days after the carrying of the resolution came the signing of a "Declaration of Independency," the document now often read during the Fourth of July's celebration. That annual event remembers the document itself rather than the act of voting for independence, and it has been recognized since 1777, when the Continental Congress first approved "a bill for materials, workmanship, &c. furnished for the fireworks on the 4 July, the sum of 102 69/90 dollars." The significance of this American holiday was even more evident when its name became fused with the adjective GLORIOUS.

Within a century's time, FOURTH OF JULY came to represent every patriotic sentiment in America. In 1867, a surge of patriotism meant that somebody "felt his Fourth of July rising too fast." The phrase, along with FOURTH-OF-JULYISM, also began to suggest jingoism. As early as 1874, patriotism began to wane: Benjamin F. Taylor, an American writer, expressed regret that "A Fourth-of-Julyism has somehow become an object of contempt."

DAY WORK

Similar disdain for Americanisms may account for the disappearance or obsolescence of many terms that were once common usage.

Today, for instance, few places celebrate PATRIOTS' DAY, and fewer still have even heard of EVACUATION DAY, much less the GLORIOUS EIGHTH OF JANUARY. A legal holiday declared in Maine and Massachusetts in 1894, Patriots' Day was celebrated on April 19 as the anniversary of the Revolutionary battle of Lexington in 1775. (Its apostrophe sometimes shifted, as in a 1948 reference to "Patriot's day in Boston," just as the apostrophe remains uncertain in "Presidents' Day.")

Evacuation Day, on the other hand, commemorated the end of the Revolutionary War, when the British troops were withdrawn from America's cities. An 1830s history of Long Island recounted that "The Evacuation day, November 25th, the day on which the British army left Brooklyn, on this island, and also the City of New York, in the year 1783, has been observed as a species of holiday on the west end of Long Island"; in Boston, Evacuation Day was the anniversary of the British departure from there on March 17, 1776. The evening of that holiday became celebrated as EVACUATION NIGHT, with its own superstitions, including an 1856 reference to "the horse-ghost, which may be seen every Evacuation night."

Many who commemorate the GLORIOUS FOURTH OF JULY have no knowledge of the Glorious Eighth of January. When General Andrew Jackson defeated the British at New Orleans in the War of 1812, an annual holiday commemorated that victory for years afterward. After a generation, though, the holiday was already disappearing in New York, and " 'The Glorious Eighth of January' . . . has almost died out as a democratic day of jubilee," reported the *New York Herald* in

1870. Jackson's victory did earn him the nickname of "Hero of New Orleans" and turned his followers into HEROITES.

JUNETEENTH, on the other hand, has been growing in popularity. June 19, 1865, is the date celebrated annually to commemorate when the slaves in Texas first learned of their emancipation. (Other areas celebrate emancipation on other dates.) It was a day far too long in coming: Lincoln's Emancipation Proclamation had been issued more than two years earlier than the Juneteenth liberation.

The times as well as the terms have changed. The wide New York avenue known as Broadway was preceded in New York history by the 1673 "Bredewegh." In 1835, the modern spelling first appeared in print, leading to the 1918 term for a person who frequents that area: "The loophound of Chicago differs visibly from the BROADWAYITE of Manhattan and the boulevardier of Paris." In light of today's inflated prices for Broadway theater, though, a 1948 prognostication in *Time* magazine proved almost as unreliable as John Adams's "Second of July," predicting that "Most show-wise Broadwayites agreed with the directors that the Met couldn't safely raise the price of its orchestra seats above the present $7.50," an amount only one-tenth of the standard ticket price in 1999.

Similarly, the 1623 COWBOY has metamorphosized during the past three centuries. The term was first applied not to Americans but to British soldiers during the Revolution. The Tory guerrilla groups that fought near New York were evaluated in an 1898 history of that war: "The cowboys were the worst kind of Tories; they went around in the bushes armed with guns and tinkling a cow-bell so as to beguile the patriots into the brush hunting for cows." In the nineteenth century the word took on overtones of brashness and recklessness; *The New Yorker* added a derisive urban definition in 1928: "Cowboy—A taxicab driver who makes speed through traffic and around fenders."

The 1920s also witnessed the term's use in derogations like

DRUGSTORE COWBOY, denoting any young man who lounges at a drugstore counter and tries to impress women, and MAIL-ORDER COWBOY, who was described in 1926 as arriving on the range "already fitted in cowboywear as he knew it from his reading and the assurances of some Middle Western storekeeper"; in his 1944 *Western Words,* Ramon F. Adams noted that "The average mail-order cowboy 'looks like he was raised on Brooklyn Bridge.' " The noun gained more big-city prominence in the 1975 song "Rhinestone Cowboy" and the 1980 John Travolta film *Urban Cowboy.*

LOSING OUT

Few American terms have had the staying power of "cowboy." Many terms, in fact, fell into the abyss represented by a Civil War term, FORGETTERY, suggesting the possibility or inevitability of forgetting. *Harper's Magazine* described an unhelpful witness in 1862: "Her memory being rather a forgettery, all she could say . . . was weighed in the balance an' come up missin'." A year later, the same magazine referred to a bad memory as "first-rate forgettery," but in spite of a brief revival a decade ago, the term has since been practically forgotten.

Sadly, too many Americanisms have fallen into forgettery, and the stories behind other terms that remain current have been lost in the mists of history. FUNGO, for example, is still used in baseball for a fly ball that is hit for fielding practice; that noun was first used after the Civil War, but nobody knows the term's origin, not even the manufacturers of the FUNGO BAT, a lightweight bat designed for hitting fly balls. Even more recent is HONKY-TONK, used since the turn of the century for a tawdry dance hall or nightclub, especially any cheap country-and-western bar. No one knows, however, why it was originally called a honky-tonk.

Other terms will probably remain entirely in obscurity. During the Civil War, for instance, the phrase THIRD MAN was current. That title of a parlor game, though, will probably remain only a title; in 1951, Mitford Mathews labeled the term as "meaning unknown" and "obsolete." In 1865, a diarist among rebel soldiers commented, "After being entertained with music and conversation we were introduced to an amusing game or play called 'scissors,' also a very laughable one called 'the third man.' We laughed over these innocent amusements until my sides were sore." Now the phrase is only known as the title of a brilliant 1949 film noir with Orson Welles, based on the novel by Graham Greene.

More valuable are terms whose meanings are known and potentially still of use in the language. GONENESS was originally used to express "exhaustion or great weariness." That noun appeared among a lexicon of Rhode Island words in 1848 and was explained as "a peculiar feeling in the stomach." Its lack of usage was already being regretted in 1879 in *The Atlantic Monthly*: "Goneness, indeed, has some humor and suggestiveness, and might be accepted as good slang if it were in sufficiently common use. It is described as being a 'woman's word'; but I have heard it from men."

Equally rare these days is the noun WANTAGE. Noah Webster's dictionary recorded the term in 1828 as meaning "deficiency; that which is wanting." Almost a century later, New York inspectors still used the term for determining the quantity of liquid missing from commercial containers. Today, though, the word could be revived to indicate more than a simple "lack" or "absence," because the richer "wantage" suggests a desire to have more. Yet the collective suffix—AGE has been renewed in the student slang of the 1980s, with such examples as FOODAGE for "a meal" and BABEAGE for "attractive women."

The noun GRASS has been at the root of other valuable Americanisms. In the nineteenth century, BETWEEN GRASS

Josing Out

AND HAY knowingly described the awkward age between childhood and adulthood. A slang collector noted in 1871 "The peculiar phrase in which the youth, who is no longer a boy, and not yet a man, is picturesquely said to be between grass and hay." This term for adolescent anxiety was sometimes used in reverse order; an 1848 list of Nantucket localisms preferred BETWIXT HAY & GRASS.

From native Americans came the poetic phrasing of AS LONG AS GRASS GROWS AND WATER RUNS. That aboriginal expression for "forever" dates back to an 1871 use in a federal report: "It had been solemnly pledged by all Departments of the government for the exclusive homes of the Indians as long as 'grass grows and water runs.' " The promise of eternity, however, like so many treaties with Native Americans, was soon broken. *Collier's Magazine* in 1907 described unfair fights for statehood that "forever laid aside the promise to the red man that he should have freedom 'as long as grass grows and water runs.' "

Not all old Americanisms may seem so colorful or worthy of reviving. Vance Randolph reported the southernism JUBER-OUS in his 1932 writings about Ozark Mountain dialect: "Th' ol' man he pondered a while, a-shakin' of his head kinder juberous." That term, however, had been given various spellings and pronunciations since 1845 and still offered little more information than its original form, "dubious." Also having little reason for revival is the 1840 verb JULEPIZE, which is merely a verb for the drinking of mint juleps. The modern hipster would probably ask for one by verbing the noun: "julep me!" And if the 1871 NEWSPAPORIALIST (an inflated term for "journalist") hasn't caught on yet, it probably never will.

Other old Americanisms, however, offer humor or playfulness to recommend their return. KADOODLE, for instance, was an inventive verb a century ago meaning "to play or sport." In 1875, a novelist used that verb in noting, "I have a little

game with a rovin' angel that comes kadoodlin' round me."
Similarly playful was a nineteenth-century pun, based on the
title of an essay by Thomas Paine in 1776, "Times That Try
Men's Souls"; an 1847 satirist wrote of a protest walk as
"These are the times that try men's SOLES."

The great outdoors led to terms more optimistic. For those
suffering from too much time indoors, WILDERNESS CURE proposed in the 1880s a way to treat illness by going camping or
living an extended time in the open air. Good fortune in the
nineteenth century came as A BREEZE OF LUCK. That colloquialism began with Davy Crockett in his 1834 autobiography: "I now began to think we had struck a breeze of luck."

Extended optimism produced other memorable phrases.
An idealist or visionary took on the 1892 identification of
RAINBOW CHASER, particularly popular in politics; a 1904
issue of a New York newspaper used a similar term in reporting that "Early in the campaign he had told his associates that
it was of no use to go rainbow chasing after Massachusetts,
Wisconsin, or Illinois." The phrase was reinforced by the popular song "I'm Always Chasing Rainbows," with its 1918
lyrics by Joseph McCarthy. The English satirist Jonathan
Swift in 1704 had introduced the combination of SWEETNESS
AND LIGHT as "the two noblest of things"; the comparable
Americanism of the nineteenth century was HONEY AND HUG
for exaggerated goodness, mentioned by a Down East writer
in 1833 who witnessed a mood swing: "All honey an' hug a
minit ago; an' now . . . what a change."

Different parts of the country have dropped useful region-
alisms from the American vocabulary. The carpeting of needles fallen from pine trees, for example, took the specific
name in Maryland of SHATS, recorded as early as the 1890s.
Farther north, however, the common term in parts of Massachusetts was DIDDLEDEES; a folklorist in 1889 remembered,
"At Hyannis, in my boyhood, it was the universal name for the
fallen pine-needles that carpet the ground in the woods." A

1942 collection of terms noted that "What you call pine leaves all depends on the section of the country in which you live. They are known as needles, spills, pins, twinkles, diddledees, straws, tags, and shats."

Finding just the right word from a varied collection became known in the 1890s as VOCABULATION. That term, based on the 1532 noun "vocabulary," referred to a person's choice or use of words (Thomas Harriot's 1585 vocabulation included the use of "merchantable" for American goods to sell). In an 1891 book, an American writer saluted "a mind . . . felicitous in vocabulation and ingenious in the construction of sentences."

ALL AMERICAN

"There is a movement in the United States today, widespread and very far-reaching in its consequences. People are seeking after a freer, healthier, happier life."

Those words could easily be mistaken for a sentiment expressed in today's newspapers or self-help magazines. Instead, they were penned almost a century ago by Laura Ingalls Wilder, who wrote the enormously popular "Little House" series of books about the personal trials and triumphs that have marked the settling of America. In her February 1911 essay "The March of Progress," she expressed the same pursuits of happiness common to current speakers of the American language.

Any complete survey of American language should acknowledge the use of AMERICAN itself. Those who first used "American" employed it after observing the lack of a satisfactory modifier form for "United States." In fact, "American" predates the formation of the nation.

Ornithologists used the form in 1730 to identify "the American goldfinch" and in 1743 for "the American partridge." Botanists also favored the term, with a gardening dictionary in 1731 indicating "A vulgar Error . . . relating to the large American Aloe, which is, that it never flowers until it is an hundred Years old," and even as the country stretched westward, "American" stood for the settled areas back East. Any cow or horse bred in the East was considered American, and therefore superior to the animals found on the plains.

American words, grand and growing, continue to be adapted and adopted with the ever-changing needs of the language, a tongue both playful and productive. (Even the variations of the word PLAY show the industriousness and inventiveness of the native expressions.) As the national character itself has grown and changed, the terms we choose and use have reflected that growth. The final word on these words must be an awareness that there is no "final word." In the endless ways of the American language, in fact, there will probably be ever more invention and never enough words.

In Play

PLAYING PASTURE a 1737 phrase, now obsolete, for what is known as a "level playing field"

PLAY HOUR another term for a school recess for games, first called for in 1774 and by 1845 known as "play spell"

PLAY POSSUM an early-nineteenth-century phrase, used in Florida in 1822 to describe the tricky creature "known to lie for several hours as if dead"

PLAY THE ADVANTAGES OVER reported in 1839 as a phrase for cheating, in use among Mississippi gamblers

PLAYED-OUT an 1859 term meaning "worn out or exhausted," clipped a decade later to simply "played"

PLAY SHARP used during the Civil War to mean "to play a trick on"

PLAY SMASH WITH an 1887 expression, perhaps from a similar Scottish expression, meaning "to affect strongly" or "to destroy"

PLAY THE HOG a turn-of-the-century term that means "to be selfish"

PLAY THE DOZENS a 1970s phrase of African-American origin for a game of exchanging insults, usually rhyming put-downs about the opponent's family

PLAYING YOU a current term from street slang for "deceiving you" or "putting one over on you"

THE LAST ROUNDUP
SOURCES

If we had a complete history of all the words which America has preserved, invented, or modified, we should possess the most revealing history conceivable of the American people.

—ROBERT L. RAMSAY

When the actor Tom Mix died in 1940, he had made more than one hundred western films, both silents and talkies. The death of the cowboy star recalled for many THE LAST ROUNDUP, a phrase from a 1932 western song about dying. "Tom Mix," began an obituary, "has laid down his honors . . . and taken the sunset trail that leads to the last roundup."

Any effort to round up all of America's words is by definition ambitious, but the notion of the ultimate American dictionary is not new. Thomas Jefferson sought such a treasury of words, although his interest extended to the entire English language in the days before the *Oxford English Dictionary*. "We want an elaborate history of the English language," Jefferson wrote in an 1825 letter. Thirteen years earlier, John Adams had expressed a nationalistic desire: "We ought to have an American Dictionary: after which I should be willing to lay a tax of an eagle a volume upon all English Dictionaries that should ever be imported." A more recent argument in favor of the great American dictionary is the observation above by Robert L. Ramsay in *The Mark Twain Lexicon.*

In the century and a half since the deaths of Jefferson and Adams, however, no singular American dictionary has emerged. Among existing dictionaries of Americanisms, the most important have included the four-volume study by Craigie and Hulbert in 1944, followed seven years later by the work of Mitford M. Mathews. To those enormously helpful references, any complete American study would need to consider the history of American slang being prepared by J. E. Lighter and the continuing work of Frederic Cassidy on the *Dictionary of American Regional English.* Producing an all-encompassing work about the American language may remain within the realm of the RAINBOW CHASERS, however.

Any unabridged dictionary of Americanisms will have a plethora of references to build upon in the millennium ahead. The following list of useful reference works is meant to be not exhaustive but rather suggestive of the multitude of volumes available about the American language.

Adams, Ramon F. *Western Words: A Dictionary of the American West.* 2d ed. Norman: University of Oklahoma Press, 1968.

Barnhart, Robert K., ed. *The Barnhart Dictionary of Etymology.* New York: H. W. Wilson, 1988.

———, et al. *Third Barnhart Dictionary of New English.* New York: H. W. Wilson, 1990.

Bartlett, John. *Familiar Quotations.* 16th ed. Revised by Justin Kaplan. Boston: Little, Brown, 1972.

Bartlett, John Russell. *Dictionary of Americanisms: A Glossary of Words and Phrases, Usually Regarded as Peculiar* to the United States. New York: Bartlett and Welford, 1848.

Berrey, Lester V., and Melvin Van den Bark. *The American Thesaurus of Slang: A Complete Reference Book of Colloquial Speech*. New York: Thomas Y. Crowell, 1942.

Blake, Fay M., and H. Morton Newman. *Verbis Non Factis: Words Meant to Influence Political Choices in the United States, 1800–1980*. Metuchen, N.J.: Scarecrow Press, 1984.

Blevins, Winfred. *Dictionary of the American West*. New York: Facts on File, 1993.

Carr, Elizabeth Ball. *Da Kine Talk: From Pidgin to Standard English in Hawaii*. Honolulu: University Press of Hawaii, 1972.

Cassidy, Frederic G. *Dictionary of American Regional English*. 3 vols., A–O. Cambridge, Mass.: Belknap Press, 1992–1996.

Chapman, Robert L. *New Dictionary of American Slang*. New York: Harper & Row, 1986.

Craigie, Sir William A., and James R. Hulbert. *A Dictionary of American English on Historical Principles*. 4 vols. Chicago: University of Chicago Press, 1944.

Cutler, Charles L. *O Brave New Words!: Native American Loanwords in Current English*. Norman: University of Oklahoma Press, 1994.

Dalzell, Tom. *Flappers 2 Rappers: American Youth Slang*. Springfield, Mass.: Merriam-Webster, 1996.

Dohan, Mary Helen. *Our Own Words*. New York: Alfred A. Knopf, 1974.

Filler, Louis. *Dictionary of American Conservatism.* New York: Philosophical Library, 1987.

Lighter, J. E. *Random House Historical Dictionary of American Slang.* Volume 1, A–G. New York: Random House, 1994.

Mathews, Mitford, ed. *A Dictionary of Americanisms on Historical Principles.* Chicago: University of Chicago Press, 1951.

Mencken, H. L. *A New Dictionary of Quotations.* New York: Alfred A. Knopf, 1946.

———. *The American Language.* 1945 ed. and two supplements. New York: Alfred A. Knopf, 1962.

Miner, Margaret, and Hugh Rawson. *American Heritage Dictionary of American Quotations.* New York: Penguin Reference, 1997.

Munro, Pamela, et al. *Slang U.: The Official Dictionary of College Slang.* New York: Harmony Books, 1989.

Murray, James A. H., et al., eds. *Oxford English Dictionary.* 13 vols. Oxford: Clarendon Press, 1889–1933.

Rawson, Hugh. *Rawson's Dictionary of Euphemisms and Other Doubletalk.* Rev. ed. New York: Crown, 1995.

Rourke, Constance. *American Humor: A Study of the National Character.* New York: Harcourt, Brace, 1931.

Safire, William. *Safire's New Political Dictionary.* New York: Random House, 1993.

Shafritz, Jay M. *The Dorsey Dictionary of American Government and Politics.* Chicago: Dorsey, 1988.

Shapiro, Fred R. *The Oxford Dictionary of American Legal Quotations.* New York: Oxford University Press, 1933.

Simpson, James B. *Simpson's Contemporary Quotations.* Boston: Houghton Mifflin, 1988.

Soukhanov, Anne H. *Word Watch: The Stories Behind the Words of Our Lives.* New York: Henry Holt, 1995.

Spears, Richard A. *Slang and Euphemism: A Dictionary.* 2d revised paperback ed. New York: Signet, 1991.

Sperber, Hans, and Travis Trittschuh. *Dictionary of American Political Terms.* New York: McGraw-Hill, 1964.

Tallman, Marjorie. *Dictionary of American Folklore.* New York: Philosophical Library, 1959.

Thornton, Richard H., ed. *An American Glossary.* 2 vols. London: St. Francis, 1912.

The United Methodist Hymnal. Nashville: United Methodist Publishing House, 1989.

Watts, Peter, ed. *A Dictionary of the Old West, 1850–1900.* New York: Wings Books, 1977.

INDEX

Index